Landmarks of the U.S.A.
OUR 51 CAPITOLS

VIEW OF THE CAPITOL, WASHINGTON, D.C. IN 1824 by Charles Burton. (The Metropolitan Museum of Art; purchase, 1942, Joseph Pulitzer Bequest)

Home Library Publishing Company
Fort Atkinson, Wisconsin

CONTENTS

The United States Capitol 3	Montana 52
Alabama 6	Nebraska 54
Alaska 8	Nevada 55
Arizona 10	New Hampshire 56
Arkansas 12	New Jersey 58
California 14	New Mexico 60
Colorado 16	New York 62
Connecticut 18	North Carolina 64
Delaware 20	North Dakota 66
Florida 22	Ohio 67
Georgia 23	Oklahoma 68
Hawaii 24	Oregon 70
Idaho 26	Pennsylvania 72
Illinois 28	Rhode Island 74
Indiana 30	South Carolina 76
Iowa 32	South Dakota 78
Kansas 34	Tennessee 80
Kentucky 36	Texas 82
Louisiana 38	Utah 84
Maine 39	Vermont 86
Maryland 40	Virginia 88
Massachusetts 42	Washington 90
Michigan 44	West Virginia 92
Minnesota 46	Wisconsin 94
Mississippi 48	Wyoming 96
Missouri 50	

Copyright © MCMLXXVI by Home Library Publishing Corporation, 917 Clarence Street, Fort Atkinson, Wisconsin 53538. All rights reserved. This book, or parts thereof, must not be reproduced in any form without permission from the publisher.

97556

BELMONT COLLEGE LIBRARY

The United States Capitol

Nothing in America attests more vividly to the strength of the Nation and the foresight of its founders than the Capitol Building of the United States. At the time the site was chosen in the new Federal City of Washington in 1791, it was planned that the building should be both serviceable and monumental.

Construction of the building in five sections covered a period of seventy years, from the laying of the cornerstone by President Washington on September 18, 1793, to the placement of the Statue of Freedom atop the present dome on December 2, 1863. To further complement the monumental majesty of the structure, the terraces were added in 1884, and the east-central portion was extended, enlarged and reconstructed in 1957-1962.

The interior is a veritable gallery of beautiful works of art, some of which took seventy-six years for completion, and many of which were the result of more than twenty-five years of work by artist Constantino Brumidi.

The first section to be constructed was the original Senate wing joining the Rotunda area on the north. Construction of this section began in 1793. President Washington officiated at the formal Masonic ceremony for laying of the cornerstone.

Despite a shortage of skills, tools and materials and difficulties between professional architects and Dr. William Thornton, young physician and amateur architect, whose design was accepted by the commission appointed to supervise planning and construction, the north wing of "Congress House" was virtually complete by autumn 1800, when the Government was moved from Philadelphia.

This first section had to accommodate the 32 Senators, 106 Representatives, the Supreme and Circuit Courts, and the Library of Congress, for not even the foundations were complete for the rest of the Capitol.

The second section was built so as to join the future central dome section on the south. Commenced in 1804, it was not completed until 1811, although the House of Representatives first occupied it in 1807. This wing was the work of Benjamin Henry Latrobe, a thoroughly trained professional architect, who collaborated closely with Thomas Jefferson after Jefferson became President.

These first two sections, the original Senate and House wings, were temporarily connected by a wooden arcade, and work had barely begun on the central section when, during the War of 1812, British troops set fire to the building on August 24, 1814. A small group of determined patriots and a rain storm were all that saved the Capitol from complete destruction.

Latrobe resumed work on the burned-out Capitol, which he called "a most magnificent ruin," in 1815. He restored the House and Senate wings, strengthening them with marble, brick, metal and sandstone. He redesigned a semicircular House Chamber and enlarged the Senate Chamber.

Resigning in 1817 after a dispute with the Commissioner of Public Buildings, Latrobe was succeeded by Charles Bulfinch, the Boston architect who had designed the Connecticut State House of 1796 and the Massachusetts State House of 1798. Bulfinch finished work on the wings in time for the Sixteenth Congress to occupy them on December 6, 1819. More notably, he completed the third and final section of the original Capitol—the central portion which joined the wings together. This included the magnificent classic-columned east and west central fronts, the Rotunda, and the low wooden copper-covered spherical dome.

In the score of years that followed, the Nation grew rapidly—and Congress with it. By 1850 it was obvious that Congress needed larger quarters, and it appropriated $100,000 to construct new chambers for both Houses as additions on the north and the south ends of the Capitol.

The new south wing was completed sufficient for occupancy by the House in 1857 and the north or Senate wing in 1859. Work had not progressed far on these extensions before it was apparent that they were going to dwarf the central dome. So, in 1855, the original dome was removed to make way for the majestic dome of today. An engineering masterpiece for the times, it has a double cast-iron shell and weighs nearly nine million pounds.

The War Between the States broke out before the new dome was finished, but at President Lincoln's insistence the work continued. He said "If people see the Capitol going on it will be a sign to them that we intend the Union shall go on."

During the Civil War the Capitol served as a military barracks, hospital, and even as a bakery when Congress was not in session. Still the work proceeded on the porticos of the new wings, which were finished by 1863.

Except for the addition of the terraces beginning in 1884, no other substantial changes were made on the Capitol until the east front extension in 1957-1962, under Architect of the Capitol J. George Stewart.

The Capitol now has sixteen and one-half acres of floor space with 540 rooms on five floors, and covers four acres of land. The Capitol grounds now total 131 acres, including the nearby legislative office buildings. The landscaping was largely the work of Frederick Law Olmsted in the mid-1870's.

Overleaf: The Nation's Capitol Building took seventy years to complete.

Jefferson Davis, President of the Confederacy, was inaugurated on the front portico of the impressive State Capitol of Alabama.

ALABAMA
THE STATE CAPITOL *Montgomery*

In 1820, one year after Alabama gained statehood, the capital was moved from Huntsville to Cahaba, where the first State Capitol building had been completed. Following a flood in 1825, the capital was moved to Tuscaloosa, where a new Capitol was completed in 1826.

In 1846, the Legislature selected Montgomery as the capital. The City of Montgomery donated a tract of land for the Capitol at the head of Dexter Avenue (then Market Street), which had been set aside for that purpose by the foresighted founder of Montgomery, Andrew Dexter. The city issued bonds and the Capitol was built at no expense to the State of Alabama. The structure, designed by Stephen Decatur Button of Philadelphia, was completed in late 1847, whereupon all records and offices were transferred to Montgomery.

On December 14, 1849, the thirtieth anniversary of Alabama statehood, a fire burned the roof of the House of Representatives. Most of the contents of the Statehouse were rescued, but the building was gutted within three hours. The Capitol was rebuilt on the foundations of the old one, of brick and plaster, and with some alterations in the original design, at a cost of $75,000. Additions, including a classic dome and stately columns, were completed in 1851.

Originally 200 feet long by 150 feet wide, the Capitol was first enlarged in 1885 by the addition of a $25,000 east wing to the rear of the building. This seventy-by-fifty-foot extension housed the Supreme Court and the State Library. Beginning in 1889, improvements were made on the Capitol Square, first with landscaping by Frederick Law Olmsted. Additional property was bought and, following an architectural competition won by Frank Lockwood, a design was adopted whereby the Capitol was to be enlarged by the addition of identical south and north wings measuring 130 by 150 feet. These were constructed in 1905 and 1911, respectively.

Included in the Lockwood additions to the Capitol was a stained glass skylight in the top of the dome. In 1937, murals painted by Roderick McKenzie depicting the history and life of Alabama were also placed in the dome.

The Lockwood design for the enlargement of the Capitol called for no alteration in the original structure, which remains as it was in 1851. The six columns on the portico are of the Corinthian style originated by Minard Lafever, while those supporting the dome are of orthodox Corinthian design. Atop the portico is the clock of the City of Montgomery, placed there in 1851.

The graceful twin spiral staircases, ascending from the entrance hall to the legislative chambers on the second floor and the visitors' gallery on the third floor, have no visible means of support. Portraits of Alabama Governors line the first floor corridors, the Governor's office, and reception rooms.

On the Capitol grounds is a handsome monument to the Confederate dead, erected by the Montgomery Ladies Memorial Association. There are also statues of Dr. J. Marion Sims, Dr. John Allen Wyeth, Jefferson Davis and Albert Patterson, and a memorial to the Marquis de Lafayette, who visited Montgomery in 1825.

At the invitation of the Alabama Secession Convention, representatives from the other seceding States met in the Senate Chamber of the State Capitol on February 4, 1861. The Confederate Congress continued to meet there until it adjourned to meet in Richmond in the summer of 1861. In the Senate Chamber the provisional and permanent Constitutions were drafted and approved and Jefferson Davis was elected President of the Provisional government of the Confederate States. He was inaugurated first President of the Confederacy on the front portico of the Capitol. Over the dome of the Capitol the first Confederate flag, the Stars and Bars, was raised by Letitia Tyler, granddaughter of President John Tyler, on March 4, 1861.

ALASKA

THE STATE CAPITOL   *Juneau*

Until 1900, Sitka (Old Archangel) was the capital of Alaska. In that year, the United States Congress moved the seat of the Territorial government to Juneau. Executive offices, however, did not leave Sitka until 1906. When Alaska's first Territorial Legislature convened in March 1913, it used rented space in the Elks Lodge, a private building in Juneau.

Located on Fourth Street between Main and Seward Streets in Juneau, the present Alaska State Capitol originally was the Federal and Territorial Building but was ceded to the State by the 1958 Alaska Statehood Act. Alaska was formally admitted to the Union on January 3, 1959.

Approximately $1 million went into the site and the building. In 1911, Congress appropriated only half the amount needed to buy the site, but Alaskans were not to be denied their eventual Capitol. Afraid the building might be indefinitely delayed, the citizens of Juneau raised enough to purchase the rest of the area, which they then gave to the Federal Government.

Designed in the offices of James A. Wetmore, supervising architect for the Federal Government, the functional six-story building was constructed by the N. P. Severin Company of Chicago.

Completion of the building, on February 2, 1931, climaxed twenty years of effort by the citizens of the Territory. Frills were at a minimum. As Alaska's Delegate to Congress, Judge James Wickersham, said at the dedication," . . . more attention is given to serviceable space and ease of access and use by a busy people . . ."

The building itself is of brick-faced reinforced concrete, with Indiana limestone used for the lower facade. The four columns of the portico, as well as the building's interior trim, are of light and dark Tokeen marble from the quarries of Alaska's Marble Island.

The Territorial Legislature thus had its first permanent chamber, and so it has remained through statehood. The second floor accommodates the State Senate and House of Representatives. The Governor's offices and the Supreme Court are on the third floor, the Superior Court on the fifth. Occupying the first floor is the Alaska Division of State Libraries. Formerly situated in the Capitol, the United States Post Office is now in the new Federal Building on Glacier Avenue.

Opposite: Tokeen Marble, a native stone, was used in the columns and interior of Alaska's Capitol. The functional six-story structure in Juneau was originally the Federal and Territorial Building.

ARIZONA

THE STATE HOUSE *Phoenix*

Situated in the center of State House Park are the Arizona State Capitol and other legislative halls of Arizona government. State House Park is located in the western section of Phoenix on 17th Avenue between Adams and Jefferson Streets.

Completed in 1900, the Capitol served Arizona during its late Territorial days and its transition to statehood in 1912. State growth increased demands on the government, necessitating the construction of an addition to the Capitol in 1918 and another in 1939. As the economy of the State surged forward after World War II, it became apparent that more space would be needed, and in 1960 new Senate and House buildings were added to the Capitol complex.

From January 22, 1864, to September 26, 1864, the Territorial Capitol was a small walled tent located at Camp Whipple in the Chino Valley near Prescott. On September 26, 1864, the Legislature convened in new quarters near the Governor's house in the town of Prescott, and it remained there until 1867, when it moved to an adobe building in Tucson. For the next ten years, most hectic in the history of the Territory, the "Old Pueblo" was the seat of government. On March 23, 1877, Prescott again became the site of the Territorial Capitol, and it remained there until February 4, 1889, when it was moved to Phoenix.

Part of the old City Hall served as the Capitol in Phoenix until occupation of the present Capitol in 1901. This building thus shows a blend of Spanish influences with modern classical Renaissance architecture.

Designed by James Riley Gordon, architect from San Antonio, Texas, the original building, now the east wing of the State House, is 182 feet long and has an extreme depth in the center of 84 feet. A dome, forty-four feet in diameter, surmounts the building, above which stands the winged "Victory Lady," sixteen feet in height. The distance from the floor to the tip of the torch is ninety-two feet, six inches.

The most striking interior architectural feature of the east wing is a central light shaft, twenty-two feet in diameter, which reaches to the dome. On each floor a railing encircles the great shaft and defines the inside border of a commodious Rotunda.

Although the main entrance is on the ground floor, the original plan, amended by reason of insufficient funds, called for an entrance by way of massive granite steps leading to the second floor.

Completed at a total cost of $135,774.29, including fixtures and incidental expenses, the original four-story structure is constructed almost entirely of Arizona materials. The first floor is of grey granite from the Salt River Mountains. The upper walls are tufa, a porous stone found in the mountains of Yavapai County. The foundation is made of malapai rock from the Camelback mountain area.

The second section of the State House, which now forms the connecting bar between the east and west wings, was designed by A. J. Gilford and erected in 1918 at a cost of $155,000. The west wing, known officially as the Department of Justice Building, was completed in 1939 at a cost of $658,441.35.

The Senate and House of Representatives wings are constructed of tufa stone, Ozark marble, Roman travertine marble and polished rainbow granite. The conforming lines of classical architecture and landscaping enhance the setting of modest, Southwestern atmosphere.

The sixteen-foot winged "Victory Lady" proudly stands on the dome of the Arizona State House. Several additions have been made to the building and the original section (center) now forms the east wing.

ARKANSAS

THE STATE CAPITOL Little Rock

The Arkansas Capitol, which resembles the National Capitol in Washington, became the seat of State government in 1911. Standing majestically amid beautifully landscaped grounds, it houses the Governor's office, the legislative chambers and other government offices.

The land on which the Capitol stands was originally acquired in 1840 for a consideration of $1,000 and consisted of approximately forty acres located on rolling land immediately west of the originally plotted portion of the city of Little Rock. Until 1901, when construction on the present Capitol began, the site was occupied by the first State Penitentiary.

Planning for the Capitol began in 1899. Actual construction on the foundation began in 1901 with the use of convict labor. In 1903, the Legislature appropriated $1 million for the building and a contract was awarded. Five years later, the funds were exhausted and the building was not completed. George W. Donaghey, who was elected Governor in 1908, promised to complete the Capitol. Under his leadership, the General Assembly appropriated additional money and employed Cass Gilbert, one of the foremost architects in America at the time, to replan and rebuild the upper part of the Capitol, including the dome.

The Legislature of 1911 was the first to convene in the new building, although the project was not entirely completed until 1914. It had cost $2.2 million and had taken fourteen years to complete.

From an architectural point of view, the Arkansas Capitol has been widely recognized as one of the finest in the country and has been used by many States as a model and guide for their Capitols. It is constructed of white native stone commonly called Batesville marble and of Indiana limestone. Its interior is of Alabama marble. The building is 420 feet long with an average width of 150 feet. The interior height of the dome from the first level is 185 feet while the top of the dome, covered in twenty-four-carat gold leaf, is 230 feet above the ground. Six magnificent bronze doors, made by Tiffany of New York, grace the entrance.

The first seat of government when Arkansas became a Territory in 1819 was at Arkansas Post, but the capital was moved to Little Rock the following year. During the Confederacy, the State Capitol was a two-story frame structure in Washington, Hempstead County.

Little Rock has had two earlier Capitols—the Territorial Capitol, where the last Territorial Legislature met in 1835, and the Old State House, which was the Capitol from 1836 to 1911. Both have been restored. Arkansas Post, the Old State House and the present

Arkansas' Capitol resembles the United States Capitol and is considered one of the Nation's finest examples of classical design.

State Capitol appeared on a 1936 U.S. postage stamp commemorating the centennial of Arkansas statehood.

The Old State House, center of almost a century of Arkansas history, is acclaimed as one of the finest examples of antebellum architecture in the South and is now used as a museum. It stands as a monument in the long road from that day of September 13, 1836, when James Conway stood in front of the Legislature and said, "Fellow citizens, the date of our existence as a free and independent State has commenced."

CALIFORNIA
THE STATE CAPITOL *Sacramento*

Set in a forty-acre park, magnificent with its wide stretches of green lawn and numerous native and exotic trees and plants, the State Capitol at Sacramento is one of the most beautiful and substantial Capitols in the United States. Within the park area, a visitor from any corner of the globe can find some species of plant life native to his homeland.

The original structure is of Roman-Corinthian design by Miner F. Butler, four stories in height and surmounted by a great dome of copper-covered wooden sheathing. At the apex of the dome is a "lantern" cupola with a small domed roof supported by twelve columns. The crowning ornament of the roof, which is covered with gold leaf, is a ball, thirty inches in diameter, made of copper and plated with gold coins. The length of the building is 320 feet, the depth 164 feet and the height (not including the dome) 94 feet. The ball on the dome is 220 feet above street level.

A most striking feature of the interior of the Capitol is the Rotunda with its domed ceiling. In the center of the Rotunda, and facing the main or west entrance of the building is a statue of Columbus making his last appeal to Queen Isabella of Spain. The walls are decorated with murals depicting historically significant periods of the State. These murals were provided for by the Legislature in 1913.

The portraits of thirty-two former Governors of the State of California are exhibited on walls of the first floor corridors. Also exhibited on these walls are the famous paintings of "The Last Spike" and "Crossing the Plains" and portraits of three of California's early-day pioneers. Replicas of the ten flags which have flown over California since 1542 are now displayed from the second floor of the Rotunda, forming a colorful circle directly under the dome.

The structure was first occupied by the Governor, State officers and the Legislature in the fall of 1869, but was not actually completed until 1874 at a cost of $2.6 million. The area covered by the original building was 52,480 square feet, and its brick foundations extend deep below the basement floor. These foundations were patterned after the ancient Spanish fortress in Panama, probably the strongest type of construction known. In 1951, a five-story addition to the Capitol was constructed at a cost of $7.6 million.

Beautification of the Capitol Park began in 1869, at about the time the Capitol was first occupied. In 1870, the grounds were graded with soil enriched with loads of river silt. During the winter of 1870-1871, some eight hundred trees and shrubs from all parts of the world were set out. This original planting consisted of some two hundred different kinds of rare plant life. Today, there are more than 40,000 trees, shrubs and flowers in the park. With more than eight hundred varieties of flora represented, ranging from subarctic to subtropical in origin, Capitol Park stands as one of the finest collections of plant life in the country.

California's first Capitol, under Spanish rule from 1770, Mexican after 1822 and American since 1846, was the famous Praesidio at Monterey. After the Constitutional Convention met in Monterey in September and October 1849, the first California Legislature convened in San Jose on December 15. A two-story adobe building there served the government when statehood was achieved in 1850. Vallejo was the next seat of government in 1852, but only for a few days. Because of poor accommodations there, the legislators moved to the Sacramento County Courthouse where they remained until the end of the session. In 1853, the Legislature convened again at Vallejo but moved the capital to Benecia after a month. Again in 1854, because of poor housing, the Legislature returned to Sacramento and a new courthouse. Except for part of 1862, when a flood forced temporary use of San Francisco's Exchange Building, the Sacramento County Courthouse served as the State Capitol until the present building was occupied in 1869.

Opposite: One significant feature of the Roman-Corinthian California Capitol is the "lantern" cupola at the apex of the copper-covered dome.

COLORADO
THE STATE CAPITOL *Denver*

Colorado's State Capitol is located in Denver, the "Mile High City" with an elevation of 5,280 feet. With its great, gold-covered dome—42 feet in diameter and rising 272 feet above the ground—it stands on a ten-acre site donated in the late 1880's by Henry C. Brown. The Corinthian architectural plan of Elijah E. Myers was selected for the structure.

The cornerstone of the building was laid with appropriate ceremonies on July 4, 1890, by the Masonic Lodge, and the building was first occupied in 1895. The last wing of the building was not completed until 1907. The original cost of the building was $2.8 million; landscaping, furnishing and other work brought the total cost to $4 million.

Seventeen years were required to complete this granite building, which contains 160 beautifully appointed rooms. More than two hundred stonecutters from Maine, Vermont, California and Texas were employed. The outer walls measure five feet thick.

The cornerstone, located at the northeast corner of the building, weighed twenty tons in its rough state. In the cornerstone are to be found a Bible, an American flag, the Constitutions of the United States and Colorado, many State records, historical data, a collection of coins and a walking stick made from a piece of the keel of "Old Ironsides."

All material used in the building is native except the steel girders and trusses and the ornamental brass. The outer walls of the Capitol are of granite, quarried near Gunnison; the foundations and wall-backing are of Fort Collins sandstone; the wainscoting and many of the interior pilasters are of Colorado onyx. The pinkish-brown onyx is complemented by floors of snow-white Colorado Yule marble.

In 1908, the dome was covered with gold leaf at a cost of $14,680. In 1950, a complete regilding job was finished with double-weight gold leaf at a cost of approximately $22,000 to the State, with the Colorado Mining Association donating forty-eight ounces of gold leaf for the project.

Murals depicting the development of Colorado adorn the walls of the first-floor Rotunda. These were the gift of the Boettcher Foundation of Colorado in 1938, and were done by Allen True of Denver, a distinguished American painter. The lyrical inscriptions that accompany each panel were composed by the noted poet and writer, Thomas Nornsby Ferril of Denver.

The floor plan is designed in the form of a Greek cross measuring 383 feet by 31.5 feet. Each face of the structure is dominated by a high Corinthian portico. Broad corridors, paved with white marble, extend from each of the four entrances to the grand staircase in the Rotunda. Immediately above, a circular well pierces the structure to the tower beneath the dome, where the inside and outside observation galleries are located. In the dome, sixteen circular stained glass windows bear the portraits of outstanding Colorado pioneers.

Offices of the Governor and his staff occupy the southwest wing of the first floor of the Capitol. Offices of the Attorney General, Auditor, Treasurer and Secretary of State are also on the first floor. These offices have been remodeled and refurnished in recent years.

The Supreme Court Chambers and Law Library are located on the second floor of the Capitol, in the north

The granite walls of Colorado's State Capitol are five feet thick. Two hundred stone cutters from four States were employed in the construction of the building which took seventeen years to complete.

and east wings. The offices of the seven Justices of the Supreme Court are on the second and third floors of the north wing. The Senate Chamber is located in the south wing of the second floor. The State House of Representatives is located near the west side of the Rotunda, on the second floor.

The Capitol exterior was cleaned in 1966 and restored to its original light grey. Outside illumination of the Capitol, which sits on a commanding hill with attractively landscaped grounds facing the front range of the Rocky Mountains, provides an impressive sight at night. A long mall sweeps to the west and ends with the Denver Municipal Building, the Greek Theater, the Public Library and the new Denver Art Museum.

For thirty-four years Colorado had to house its Territorial and State government in temporary, scattered, rented quarters, first in Denver, then in Colorado City (now a part of Colorado Springs), back in Denver, then in Golden City. Finally, by vote of the people on November 8, 1881, Denver was made the permanent capital of the Centennial State.

Statues of Connecticut's colonial leaders and men of letters adorn all four exterior walls of the elaborate statehouse in Hartford. The building is the only Gothic-style Capitol in the United States.

CONNECTICUT

THE STATE CAPITOL *Hartford*

Hartford has been Connecticut's seat of government since it broke off from the Massachusetts Bay Colony and its first General Court convened in 1637, although the city was a joint capital with New Haven from 1701 until 1875. Of the Legislature's many previous homes in both cities, only Hartford's Old State House, designed by Charles Bulfinch and used from 1796 to 1879, is still preserved. It is now a museum.

The present Capitol, a Gothic-type structure capped by a golden dome and located adjacent to the beautiful forty-one acre Bushnell Park, became the official seat of Connecticut's State government in 1879, although the building was not actually completed until 1880. Its architect was Richard Marshall Upjohn.

The exterior is of marble from the old quarries at East Canaan, Connecticut, and granite from Westerly, Rhode Island. The interior columns are also of marble and granite quarried in Connecticut, Maine, Vermont and Rhode Island. The floor designs are famous for their beauty. The woodwork finish is oak, black walnut and ash.

The entire cost of the building was $2,532,524.43. The cost of the furniture was an additional $100,000.

Within the Capitol are the chambers and offices of the General Assembly, the headquarters of the State's elected officials and several commission offices. On the north and east sides of the exterior, historic scenes are depicted in bas-relief, while statues of colonial leaders and men of letters are found on all four exterior sides of the building at the second- and third-floor levels.

In addition to several statues, there are on the grounds "The Petersburg Express," a mortar relic of the Civil War, at the entrance to the southeast driveway, and on the north terrace, two nine-inch Dahlgren guns once used on the *Hartford*, Admiral Farragut's flagship in the famous Civil War naval battle at Mobile Bay. The figurehead and a model of the *Hartford* are in the north lobby.

The House of Representatives is on the second floor. The traditional system of unit representation, whereby each town sent either one or two representatives to the Connecticut House of Representatives, was abolished in favor of a plan creating 177 assembly districts with one representative each, effective with the 1966 State election. The House is equipped with an electronic roll call system and each desk has its own microphone. Particularly eye-catching are the beautiful, multihued, stained glass windows and the blue carpet colorfully emblazoned with the armorial bearings of the State.

The Senate Chamber is on the third floor. Visitors will be interested in the circular arrangement of the thirty-six Senators' desks in the chamber. By tradition, the Senators refer to themselves as members of "The Circle." In contrast to the blue of the House, the carpeting in the Senate is a deep red, which harmonizes with the wall paneling and desks.

The ornately carved chair on the rostrum from which the Lieutenant Governor of Connecticut presides over the State Senate was made from the celebrated "Charter Oak," the giant tree which once concealed the Charter of Connecticut from the British.

The Hall of Flags is on the first floor. On September 17, 1879, the battle flags of Connecticut's own Civil War regiments were moved from the Old State Arsenal to a permanent museum in the new State Capitol. Other mementos of the State's illustrious past are also located in the Hall of Flags.

A bronze statue of Nathan Hale stands in the first-floor corridor of the Capitol, facing the east entrance. Its marble base carries the immortal words uttered by the young patriot as he was about to be hanged: "I only regret that I have but one life to lose for my country."

DELAWARE
LEGISLATIVE HALL *Dover*

Legislative Hall replaced the Old State House which had served Delaware since 1792. The Capitol retains the colonial atmosphere appropriate to the heritage of the Nation's first State.

Delaware's present Capitol was completed in 1933, replacing the Old State House, which had served as the seat of State government since 1792. Known as Legislative Hall, the new building, designed by E. William Martin of Wilmington, emphasizes Georgian colonial architecture. It is constructed of handmade brick and follows the style of the old Capitol.

Legislative Hall is located east of The Green in Dover and is easily recognized by its formal beauty, highlighted with gables, chimneys and a three-tiered tower.

The interior of the building is reminiscent of the eighteenth century with the woodwork and other appointments following the theme of that era. This is particularly noticeable in the Governor's office suite, which is furnished in eighteenth-century décor. Two paintings by Thomas Sully hang in the Governor's office. Both are portraits of Delaware-born heroes of the War of 1812, Commodore Thomas MacDonough and Commodore Jacob Jones. The walls of the hallways of Legislative Hall hold other portraits of distinguished Delawarians, including many World War II heroes.

The House and Senate Chambers are on the first floor along with offices for members of the Legislature and meeting rooms for various committees. The Governor's offices as well as the office of the Lieutenant Governor and Secretary of State are on the second floor. The Legislative Reference Bureau is located temporarily in the basement.

Both the north and south ends of the building have been extended—new construction carefully preserving the colonial atmosphere of the building. The additional space is used for offices and conference rooms.

Partly because of its name, but primarily because of its long service, the Old State House remains to many Delaware citizens the State's "Capitol." It stands on the site of the first Kent County Courthouse, erected in 1722, which became the State Capitol in 1777. Originally built from 1787 to 1792, the Old State House was expanded several times until it was no longer possible to keep up with the space needs of the government. It is still used for some State offices but will eventually be restored as a landmark in the history of Delaware, first State to ratify the U.S. Constitution.

A. K. Pfister

FLORIDA
THE STATE CAPITOL *Tallahassee*

The offices of Florida State government are located in a beautiful landscaped section of Tallahassee known as Capitol Center—and the focal point is the Capitol building itself. A handsome, striking edifice, its architecture follows classic Greek styling, including six Doric columns. Also attractive is a high dome, with still another dome atop an arch-supported cupola.

Its cornerstone was laid in 1826, but because of financial difficulties the building was not completed until 1845, the year Florida was admitted to the Union. It was remodeled in 1901 and at that time the north and south ends were enlarged and the dome was erected. Twenty years later, the Capitol was enlarged a second time when the east and west wings were built. In 1938, a new north wing was completed, and a new south wing was added nine years later. However, the center is still the same brick building, dating back to 1845, which replaced the log cabins used originally by the Florida Territorial Legislature.

The Capitol has been the scene of historic moments in both State and American history. Here, in 1861, the Secession Convention declared Florida's withdrawal from the Federal Union and established the independent Republic of Florida. Later, Florida became a member of the Confederate States of America. It also housed three Constitutional Conventions—in 1865, 1868 and 1885. The last date was when the present State Constitution was adopted. In this same building, in 1876, the Florida Canvassing Board counted in the votes of four Republican electors, thus assuring the election of Rutherford B. Hayes as President of the United States.

Tallahassee, a tiny Indian village, was originally selected as the capital of the State because of its location. It was midway between St. Augustine, the capital in 1819, when the U.S. purchased the area from Spain, and Pensacola where the second session of the Territorial Legislature was held in 1822.

The focal point of Capitol Center in Tallahassee is this handsome building designed after the classic Greek style. The Secession Convention met here in 1861 to declare Florida's withdrawal from the Union and establish the State as an independent republic.

GEORGIA

THE STATE CAPITOL *Atlanta*

The present Georgia Capitol building in Atlanta was begun October 26, 1884; the cornerstone was laid September 2, 1885; and the massive building of Indiana limestone was finished and occupied June 15, 1889.

First home for the Georgia Legislature, both as a Colony and as a revolutionary State, was Savannah. The British capture of Savannah in 1778 forced successive moves to Augusta, Heard's Fort, Ebenezer and Augusta again. The government returned to Savannah in 1783, but during that session once more chose Augusta, where the U.S. Constitution was ratified January 2, 1788. After moving to the town of Louisville in 1796, the Legislature erected its first permanent Capitol. This served until the move in 1807 to the small middle-Georgia town of Milledgeville, capital for the next sixty years.

Construction of the Capitol in Atlanta followed a decision by the Legislature, confirmed by a popular election in 1877, to fix the seat of government in that city. The first Capitol in Atlanta, 1868-1889, was the Kimball Opera House.

Because of a shortage of funds, money for construction of the new Capitol in Atlanta was not provided until 1883, when the General Assembly appropriated $1 million for the project. The legislative act stipulated that the cost should not exceed that amount.

Ironically, because of the General Assembly's strict limitation on expenditures, the Capitol was built not of Georgia marble, which was in abundant supply in the State, but of less expensive Indiana limestone. Georgia marble was used, however, for the interior finish of walls, floors and steps.

The style of architecture of the Capitol is classical Renaissance. Its greatest length, north and south, is 347 feet, and the greatest depth through the center is 272 feet. The open Rotunda extends upward 237 feet from the second floor.

The Byzantine dome of the Capitol is seventy-five feet in diameter and is surmounted by a fifteen-foot statue. As part of a renovation which took place in 1957 and 1958, forty-three ounces of native Georgia gold were donated by the citizens of Dahlonega and of Lumpkin County and were applied in the form of gold leaf to the dome. The gold dome of the Capitol is an impressive part of the burgeoning Atlanta skyline.

A fifteen-foot statue crowns the Byzantine dome of Georgia's Capitol, which is styled along classical Renaissance lines.

Above: Iolani Palace, the royal residence after 1882, remained the seat of government when Hawaii achieved Territorial status.

Below: The unique cultural and natural history of the Island State inspired the contemporary design of the new Capitol.

HAWAII
THE NEW CAPITOL *Honolulu*

One of the initial acts of the Legislature after Hawaii achieved statehood on March 18, 1959, was to appropriate funds for the design of a new Capitol to be erected opposite Iolani Palace, the existing Capitol. Begun in 1965, the legislative chambers and offices were used during the 1968 legislative session. The balance of the project is scheduled to be completed in the early summer of 1969.

The new Capitol, while highly functional in design, manifests symbolism of both the cultural and the natural aspects of Hawaii. From a distance, it suggests an ancient Hawaiian great house. At close range, it appears to rise out of a lovely moat—symbolic of the Pacific Ocean—on tall columns which resemble Royal Hawaiian palm trees. The exterior walls of the legislative chambers slope upward in the manner of a volcanic cone. The impression of the volcano, so characteristic of the origin and geology of Hawaii, is further enhanced by the upward view from the lobby. Here, one can look up at the sky through the huge conical opening, which exposes the lobby to the natural elements of Hawaii's tropical climate.

From the upper floors of the Capitol, especially from the Governor's offices, the full panorama of Oahu is visible: Iolani Palace, Pearl Harbor, downtown Honolulu, the mountains and the sea. This view will be enhanced as the total Capitol development is completed. The Palace will be restored and the grounds will be expanded to create broad green spaces throughout the seat of government.

Iolani Palace, the old Capitol, the only royal residence in the United States, was built by King Kalakaua. The cornerstone was laid on December 31, 1879, and on December 27, 1882, the King took up official residence. The first Iolani Palace, built in 1845 of coral blocks, occupied this same site—once a section of a Hawaiian temple which was destroyed in the early 1800's. It was used for royal receptions and other state occasions by Kings Kamehameha III, IV and V and Kings Lunalilo and Kalakaua.

The present Palace reflects the European influence brought back by Kalakaua from a trip around the world. Built of concrete block and brick with cement facing, it measures forty by one hundred feet. Its tower rises to seventy-six feet. The name "Iolani" may be translated "Bird of Heaven" and signifies to Hawaiians the Supreme Being above all gods. It was a sacred name in old Hawaii and was given to both Kamehameha II and Kamehameha IV.

Upon Kalakaua's death in 1891, his sister, Liliuokalani, became Queen and lived in the Palace until the overthrow of the monarchy in 1893. Two years later she spent nine months as a prisoner in the Palace, following an insurrection that attempted to restore her to the throne.

The Palace became the executive building of the republic and remained the seat of government after Territorial status was achieved in 1900. The House of Representatives met in the Throne Room and the Senate in the State Dining Room, while the Governor and Lieutenant Governor occupied what had been the royal bedrooms on the second floor.

The Governor's office and both houses of the Legislature retained use of the Palace's rooms while awaiting completion of the new Capitol. When restored as it was in the days of the monarchy, Iolani Palace will live on as a vivid representation of Hawaii's history and cultural preservation.

IDAHO

THE STATE CAPITOL *Boise*

Located in the heart of Boise in the center of two beautifully landscaped city blocks at the end of Capitol Boulevard, the Idaho State Capitol commands an impressive view of the capital city.

Idaho Territory was organized March 4, 1863, from what are now the States of Idaho and Montana and a large portion of the State of Wyoming. Lewiston was the capital until the second Legislature designated Boise in May 1865. Idaho was reduced to its present boundaries in 1868, and on July 3, 1890, it was admitted to the Union as the forty-third State.

A small frame building served the Territorial Legislature in Lewistown. In Boise, the Legislature occasionally met in such places as the Overland Hotel or at Hart's Exchange, later known as the Central Hotel. A more substantial building was used as the Capitol from late 1886 until 1912.

By act of March 3, 1905, provision was made for a Capitol Building Board. The Governor, Secretary of State, State Treasurer and two public-spirited citizens became the Capitol Building Commission. The original appropriation was only $250,000, because much of the cost of the building was to have been paid from the sale of public lands allowed to the State by the Idaho Admission Act. The Capitol Commission decided to serve as its own contractor. Work began on the first floor during the summer of 1906.

The problem of obtaining sandstone for the outside finish was solved when the Commission purchased a stone quarry at Tablerock in October of that year. The site was convenient for use of prison labor and the Commission regarded the land as a sound investment.

The original design for the State Capitol, following the same classical style of architecture as the National Capitol, was only for the central section and the dome. The construction of it took more than six years. In August 1912, a contract was awarded for the design of wings for the building. Actual construction of the wings was delayed until the Legislature authorized funds for completion in 1919. The entire structure was finished at the end of 1920.

When completed, the building cost $2,098,455, with another $130,833 for furnishings. It covers 50,646 square feet, with floor space totaling 201,720 square feet. The height of the building, including the bronze eagle atop the dome, is 208 feet.

Alaskan marble was used on the floors, staircases and interior ornamentation, while the inside walls are of

Vermont marble. The Rotunda proper has two circular promenades. The one on the fourth floor is sixty feet in diameter and the one on the third floor eighty feet. It is of unique construction in that it is supported by columns. The fourth floor features 301 life-like specimens of birds. On the main floor is a gilded statue of George Washington on horseback, carved from native yellow pine.

The House and Senate Chambers are located on the third floor on the east and west sides, respectively.

On the fiftieth anniversary of Idaho statehood in 1940, the Capitol building was honored by being depicted on a U.S. postage stamp.

The magnificent Idaho Capitol located in the heart of Boise commands a sweeping view of the city and the surrounding mountains.

ILLINOIS
THE STATE CAPITOL *Springfield*

The handsome domed building which is the State Capitol of Illinois is actually the sixth Capitol the State has had since it was welcomed into the Federal Union in 1818. Construction began in 1868 but was not completed until 1888, twenty years later, although the various departments of the government started occupying the structure in 1876. The cost skyrocketed far above the original figure of $3 million, winding up at approximately $4.5 million.

Occupying nine acres of land, the building, which measures 379 by 268 feet, is in the shape of a Latin cross. The focal point is a vast dome, which rises to a height of 361 feet, with still another forty-four feet to the tip of its flagstaff. It is topped with a red beacon as a warning light for approaching aircraft. The dome is supported by walls seventeen feet at the base. The foundation, ninety-two feet in diameter, sits on solid rock. Farther below this strata is a rich vein of coal.

The Rotunda walls and arches are solid stone, faced with Missouri red granite. This material also was used for the polished columns on the Rotunda's third floor. The bases of these columns are blue granite and Tuckahoe marble. Various kinds of marble are used extensively throughout the interior, including the grand stairway. The interior is very impressive with marble mosaics, historical murals, oil paintings and statuary.

As visitors enter the Rotunda their eyes go to a bronze statue of "Illinois Welcoming the World" which stands at the center of the Rotunda floor. The statue was first displayed at the Columbian Exposition in Chicago in 1893. Branching off from the Rotunda are two stories of executive offices in the four wings of the building.

The present Capitol building was preceded by five other such structures, with only its immediate predecessor being in Springfield. The others were located in Kaskaskia and Vandalia.

Kaskaskia served as the first capital when Illinois was organized as a Territory and continued until 1820, two years after Illinois became a State, when Vandalia was selected as the new capital. The first two Capitols are no longer in existence. Both the State House and the city of Kaskaskia have been swallowed up by the rampaging Mississippi, while the original building at Vandalia was destroyed by fire in 1823 and was replaced by a brick structure.

However, pressure for a more centrally located capital was growing. The General Assembly called for a popular vote to choose from six sites. The subsequent vote in 1834 was so close for three cities—Alton, Springfield and Vandalia—that the result was never announced, and Vandalia remained as the capital.

Some citizens, including Abraham Lincoln, mounted a heavy campaign to move the capital to Springfield. Finally in 1837 they were successful, despite the efforts of Vandalians who razed the old building and built a new $16,000 State House in the summer of 1836 while the Legislature was in recess.

The cornerstone for the first building in Springfield was laid on July 4, 1837, and operations began there in 1839, a year before the officially set date. It took sixteen years to complete and ended up costing twice as much as its orginally estimated $130,000. It remained as the Capitol until 1876 when the State government moved to the present structure. The old building was used as the Sangamon County Courthouse. Recently restored to its appearance in Lincoln's day, at a cost of $7 million, it was dedicated in 1968 as a Lincoln shrine.

Opposite: Illinois' General Assembly convenes in this handsome structure built in the shape of a Latin cross. The vast dome, rising to a height of 361 feet, is supported by walls 17 feet at the base.

INDIANA
THE STATE HOUSE *Indianapolis*

When Indiana became a State in 1816, Congress donated four square miles of land on which to build a capital city, the land to be selected from those sections of the public land remaining unsold. The grant further provided that proceeds from the sale of lots within the four square miles could be used to defray the costs of erecting the Capitol and other public buildings.

In 1820, a commission appointed by the Legislature selected a site at the juncture of the White River and Fall Creek for the new capital. The site was approved by the Legislature the next year and, after much debate, the proposed city was named Indianapolis, meaning Indiana City. In April 1821, the work of laying out the city began. One of the surveyors, Alexander Ralston, had been employed by the French engineer, Pierre L'Enfant, in mapping out Washington, D.C., and at his suggestion the city was to be one mile square, with streets crossing at right angles and four wide avenues pointing to a circle in the center.

The Capitol grounds, known as The State House Square and Governor's Circle, near the center of Indianapolis, are cited in the Constitution of Indiana and by that authority are never to be leased or sold. The latter plot is the site of the famous Indiana Soldiers' and Sailors' Monument. The second of two State Capitols occupies State House Square.

The State government moved from a small two-story stone structure in Corydon to a very similar building, the Marion County Court House, in Indianapolis in 1825. It occupied the first specially constructed Capitol in Indianapolis from 1835 to 1878.

The present State Capitol is a classic Corinthian-design four-story building of Indiana limestone with executive offices of the State government, including those of the Governor, Lieutenant Governor, Secretary of State, Treasurer, Auditor, Attorney General and government agencies. It also contains the chambers of the House of Representatives, the Senate, and the Supreme and Appellate Courts.

Construction on the present Capitol began on October 12, 1878, on the site of the former Capitol and was completed ten years later on October 2, 1888. Two architects were engaged in its building—Edwin May from 1878 to 1880 and Adolf Scherer from 1880 to 1888. The cost was $1,980,969, just under its $2 million appropriation.

The distinguishing feature of the Capitol is the massive dome, 72 feet in diameter and rising from the center to a height of 234 feet. The dome is constructed of stone and rests on eight great columns of Maine granite. Eight Italian Carrara marble statues of heroic size placed within the Rotunda at the third floor level represent Law, Oratory, Agriculture, Commerce, Justice, Liberty, History and Art. On each floor a corridor sixty-eight feet wide extends the entire length of the building and is illuminated from attic to basement by ample skylights. A double row of marble columns, piers and pilasters support the upper structure.

Memorials to many Hoosier heroes are placed inside the Capitol and on its nine acres of grounds. A statue of Oliver P. Morton, Governor of Indiana from 1861 to 1867, stands outside the east entrance to the building. On the southeast corner is a statue of Thomas A. Hendricks, Governor from 1873 to 1877 and Vice President of the United States in 1885. In front of the south entrance is a bust of Robert Dale Owen, author, statesman, philanthropist and active campaigner for the rights of women. Just west of the south wing of the building is a bust of Christopher Columbus. Portraits of Indiana's Governors line the fourth-floor corridor.

The massive stone dome rising from the center of the Hoosier Capitol building is supported by eight wide granite columns.

IOWA
THE STATE HOUSE *Des Moines*

Created as a separate Territory in 1838, Iowa moved its capital from Burlington to Iowa City in 1842. Later that year, the Territorial Legislature occupied the first permanent Capitol—now the administration building of the University of Iowa—remaining there until 1857.

In 1854, the Fifth General Assembly of the State decreed a location "within two miles of the Raccoon forks of the Des Moines River" for its new Capitol in Des Moines. The exact spot was chosen when Wilson Alexander Scott gave the State nine and a half acres with a hilltop view of the countryside. A group of Des Moines citizens built a temporary Capitol (later bought by the State) near the present location of the Soldiers' and Sailors' Monument. In use from 1857, it was eventually destroyed by fire, but in the meantime the permanent Capitol was being planned and built. In 1870, the General Assembly established a Capitol Commission to employ an architect, choose a plan and proceed with work on the permanent Capitol. The frugal legislators, however, stipulated that the cost was not to exceed $1.5 million of available funds and that the tax rate was not to be increased. Unfortunately, this proved uneconomical, for soon after the cornerstone was laid in 1871, a hard winter caused the cheap materials of the foundation to crumble. Almost all of the stone work had to be redone. A new commission obtained adequate appropriations and a new cornerstone was placed in 1873. Work was finished in 1886 at a cost of $2,873,294.59.

The modified Romanesque building was dedicated in January 1884, with the General Assembly in session. The executive offices were occupied the next year, and the Supreme Court's chamber was dedicated in 1886.

In 1902, in order to modernize and repair the building, a third Capitol Commission was created. While work proceeded, a disastrous fire in the north wing, January 4, 1904, ruined the House Chamber and damaged other offices. The commission restored the building, purchased paintings and mosaics and redecorated almost all the interior. The original decorations are still in the Senate.

The commanding feature of the Capitol is the central towering dome. This was constructed of steel and stone and covered with gold. The gold leaf was replaced in recent years at a cost of $79,938. The dome is surmounted by a lookout lantern reached by long, winding stairs, and a finial 275 feet above the ground floor. The Rotunda beneath the dome is sixty-seven feet in diameter. Four smaller domes of simple design rise from the four corners of the Capitol. The pediment over the front entrance discloses a fine piece of allegorical sculpture. The building itself measures 364 by 247 feet.

Materials for the Statehouse came from Iowa and neighboring States: stone for the basement was quarried in Johnson County; stone for the main structure from Carroll County in Missouri; steps, columns and other parts from Anamosa, Iowa, Ohio, Minnesota and Illinois. Imported and domestic marble of twenty-nine kinds was used in the interior; and the wood used was nearly all from Iowa forests of black walnut, cherry, catalpa, butternut and oak.

A hilltop overlooking the Iowa countryside provides a lovely site for the Romanesque-style State House in Des Moines.

The Senate Hall is 58 feet long, 91 feet wide, and 41.9 feet high. It is finished in marble, white oak and scagliola. Furnishings are mahogany. The figures in the ceiling represent Industry, Law, Agriculture, Peace, History and Commerce. The Hall of the House of Representatives, finished in marble, scagliola, and black walnut, is 74 by 91.4 feet, and 47.9 feet in height.

Over the main stairway hangs "Westward," a large painting by Edwin H. Blaskfield, signifying the settling of Iowa. Above this are six Venetian mosaics representing Defense, Charities, Education and the Executive, Legislative and Judicial branches. The Rotunda features many battle flags and twelve statues of Art, History, Science, Law, Fame, Industry, Peace, Commerce, Agriculture, Victory, Truth and Justice.

KANSAS
THE STATE HOUSE *Topeka*

Kansas was admitted to the Union in 1861, and Topeka was selected as the capital city of the State in an election held that November. Several buildings served as meeting places for the House and Senate during the following eight years.

At the legislative session of 1866, a plan was adopted for a State House. The east wing, started that year, was completed in 1873, using stone from Geary County. The other three wings were built of stone from Cottonwood Falls. The first legislative session in the building was held in 1870, although work on the west wing did not begin until 1879.

By the summer of 1880, the west wing was practically enclosed. The House of Representatives of 1881 met in the unfinished new hall for that session, while State offices were occupied during the same years. The total cost of the west wing was only about $300,000 against $500,000 for the east wing, which was very much inferior to the former in material and workmanship.

Construction of the main building was authorized in 1881. In 1892, rooms were temporarily finished and used on the ground floor of the south wing. The completed building cost the State of Kansas $3,200,588.92, the last of which was paid by the State in March 1903.

The building measures 399 feet north and south, 386 feet east and west, and 304 feet to the top of the dome. There are 296 steps from the top of the building to the top of the dome.

At one time, some State offices had handsome porcelain bathtubs and washstands of pure white marble, put in during the Populist administration, which also added the Georgian marble in the third-floor Rotunda.

The wainscoting in the center of the building on the first floor is of Tennessee marble, in the west corridor of Mandual tile, and in the east corridor of Georgian marble. The large upper panels in wainscoting on the second floor are built of Siena and Lambertin marble from Italy. The Governor's offices are on this floor and are finished in white mahogany from Mexico.

The Senate Chamber and the House of Representatives are located on the third floor. The large panels on the wall of the Senate Chamber are Mexican onyx. All of the wood in the Senate is walnut, except for the solid cherry desks and chairs of the Senators. The material around all of the doors in the Senate Chamber is beautifully cut Tennessee marble. The marble in the House is from Tennessee, and the wainscoting on the east wall is made of various kinds of imported marble, trimmed with Italian Carrara, with panels of Brocelian marble and Belgian green marble in the base of the handsome columns.

The principal features of the dome interior are the four large mural paintings near the top. The east panel represents Religion, Knowledge and Temperance; the north panel, Plenty; west panel, Peace; and the south, Power.

There are sixteen acres of land inside the sidewalk line of the Capitol grounds.

The Kansas State House, built entirely of native stone in the popular classical style, is 304 feet high with 296 steps leading from the top of the building to the top of the dome.

KENTUCKY
THE STATE CAPITOL *Frankfort*

Kentucky's classic Capitol is the fourth erected in Frankfort. While a district of Virginia, Kentucky held nine conventions in Danville, finally drawing up a State Constitution there in 1792. The Constitutional Convention designated Lexington as the site of the first General Assembly, which, meeting in a log building in that town in June 1792, chose Frankfort as the permanent seat of government.

The first Capitol there, built in 1793-1794, burned in 1813; its replacement, completed in 1816, suffered a similar fate in 1824. The third, modeled in part after a Greek temple to Minerva, was finished in 1830. This Old State House is now the home of the Kentucky Historical Society and contains the State's archives, a museum of history and a library.

Impetus for a new Capitol came when it was determined that the Federal Government would give the State at least a million dollars for Civil War and Spanish-American War claims. The 1904 General Assembly matched the amount and appointed a Capitol Building Commission. At a special session the next year, the Legislature chose a thirty-four acre site in South Frankfort. Ground was broken that May and the cornerstone laid in June 1906.

Partially occupied in 1909 and dedicated on June 1, 1910, the new Capitol cost $1,820,000, which was widely regarded as a great bargain for a public building. That figure included land, construction, and furnishings. Remarkably, only one piece of power-driven machinery, a steam concrete mixer, was used; all other equipment, including a crane and steel bender, was hand operated.

Surrounded by a stone terrace, the three-story Capitol has oolitic limestone facing above a base of Vermont granite. The building is 403 feet from east to west, 180 feet north to south; its Rotunda measures fifty-seven feet in diameter. The outer walls are graced with seventy ornamental Ionic columns of Bedford stone.

Over the north entrance, the sculptured pediment shows Kentucky as a heroic woman, standing before the chair of State and attended by the personified figures of Progress, History, Plenty, Law, Art and Labor.

Inside, thirty-six Vermont granite columns flank the long nave, adorned with oil paintings in lunettes and at each end with a mural scene from the life of Daniel Boone. The east mural shows explorer Boone and his party first viewing the Bluegrass Region, while at the west end of the nave he is shown negotiating with the Indians for the purchase of Kentucky. The interior walls and stairway are of white Georgia marble, the floors of light Tennessee and dark Italian marble.

There is much French influence within. The Rotunda, dome and lantern are copied after the Hotel des Invalides, site of Napoleon's tomb in Paris. Stairways, balustrades and bannisters resemble those of the Paris Opera, while the State Reception Room was inspired by Marie Antoinette's drawing room in the Grand Trianon Palace at Versailles.

The House and Senate Chambers feature scagliola—ornamental plastering with a marble-like effect. Both the legislative halls and the Court of Appeals are rich in mahogany.

Bordering the Kentucky River, the well-landscaped Capitol grounds include the Governor's Mansion and the Capitol Annex.

Opposite: Seventy ornamental Ionic columns grace the exterior walls of the State Capitol in Frankfort, Kentucky.

LOUISIANA

THE STATE CAPITOL *Baton Rouge*

Louisiana's State Capitol at the time of construction was the tallest building in the South. Thirty-four stories, 450 feet in height, it was erected on the site of the old campus of Louisiana State University in Baton Rouge, which now is converted into twenty-seven acres of landscaped grounds. The Capitol was built in fourteen months, from January 1931 to March 1932, at a cost of $5 million. It was designed by Architects Weiss, Drefous and Seiferth of New Orleans.

The Capitol's elaborateness lies in intricate and costly artistic interpretations of the State itself. The story of Louisiana is the decorative theme of every detail and object that went into the edifice. Yet the building is efficiently designed and provides 249,000 square feet (nearly six acres) of floor space for governmental agencies.

In front of the building, broad steps of Minnesota granite are flanked by statuary groups called "The Patriots" and "The Pioneers." The forty-eight steps arranged in four groups are each inscribed with the name of a State, the thirteen of the lower groups representing the original colonies. The remaining steps are inscribed with the States' names in order of their admission to the Union, the State of Louisiana being the eighteenth in 1812.

The Memorial Hall is the most magnificent chamber of the building. Of huge proportions, 35 by 120 feet, the hall has a floor of polished lava from Mount Vesuvius. In the center of the floor is a huge bronze plaque on which is outlined in relief a map of Louisiana. The plaque is ten feet in diameter and weighs 3,290 pounds. The names of Louisiana's sixty-four parishes (counties) are carved around the border. Leading resources and products of each parish are also depicted.

From the observation tower, almost 450 feet above the ground, it is possible on a clear day to see the surrounding country for a distance of twenty miles. The Mississippi River, winding out of the north, passes the Capitol near its base and disappears around a great bend into the south.

Baton Rouge did not become Louisiana's capital city until 1849. The first seat of government under the State and its predecessor Territory of Orleans was New Orleans, where the Spanish regime's Government House was used until 1828. The capital was Donaldsonville from 1828 to 1831 but then reverted to New Orleans. During the Confederate and Reconstruction periods the government was situated in Opelousas, Shreveport and New Orleans before returning to Baton Rouge.

Every decorative detail in the skyscraper Capitol
at Baton Rouge illustrates an aspect of the Creole State's History.

MAINE
STATE HOUSE *Augusta*

The State House of Maine originally resembled the Boston State House. In 1909, it was redesigned in the Greek Renaissance style and now retains only the "Bulfinch Front" of the original structure.

Citizens of Portland built Maine's first State House there in 1820 when Maine was separated from Massachusetts and granted statehood. In 1827, Augusta was designated the capital, and in 1829, the cornerstone of the present State House was laid.

The State House, designed by the eminent Boston architect, Charles Bulfinch, and built of granite from nearby Hallowell, Maine, was completed in 1831. The Legislature first met there on January 4, 1832. Originally estimated to cost $80,000, the Capitol, after landscaping and furnishing, actually required $139,000.

Bulfinch's design for the Maine Capitol was similar to that for his earlier Boston State House. This is still evident in the columns-over-arches treatment of their front porticos. The architect did not settle for copying himself, for each design displays its own individuality.

In 1909-1910, the State House was redesigned by G. Henri Desmond in Greek Renaissance style and rebuilt almost completely. Hardly more than the "Bulfinch front" was retained from the original structure. Its length was doubled to three hundred feet. A 185-foot dome, crowned by W. Clark Noble's copper figure of Wisdom, covered with gold, gives the building imposing height. Spacious wings were constructed for the House of Representatives on the north and the Senate and executive chambers on the south.

The State Archives offices are located on the second floor of the Capitol. The State Library occupies the first two floors of the north wing, while the State Museum is on the first floor south.

The Museum features examples of the minerals, plants and animals found in Maine, as well as many items from the State's history. One display in particular is most unusual: Live land-locked salmon and brook trout swim in a stream, across which stretches a replica of an old-fashioned covered bridge.

Along the Capitol's corridors hang portraits of distinguished sons of Maine, and battle flags are exhibited in the Rotunda.

The State House's beautifully landscaped grounds, covering thirty-four acres, reach to the Kennebec River, an appropriate setting for this distinguished building.

MARYLAND
STATE HOUSE *Annapolis*

The Maryland State House in Annapolis is an imposing edifice with a prominent place in American history. This building, the third Capitol to occupy the commanding site of the town's highest point, was begun in 1772 at a cost of 7,500 pounds sterling. The large, unique wooden dome, made without nails and held together with wooden pegs, was added after the War of Independence.

Although the General Assembly no longer meets in the original section, it is the oldest State Capitol still fulfilling its original purpose. Since 1780 only one session of the Maryland Legislature has been held elsewhere; in 1861 the session was moved about seventy miles west to Frederick because of the strong Confederate sentiment of the people of southern Maryland.

In its earliest years the State House was the scene of events of major historical importance. Here, as the American Revolution was drawing to a close, the Continental Congress met, with Annapolis serving as the capital of the United States from late November 1783 until June 1784.

General George Washington came to Annapolis on December 23, 1783. In the room now on display as the Old Senate Chamber, he appeared before Congress and resigned his commission as Commander-in-Chief of the Continental Army. Thomas Jefferson, author of the Declaration of Independence, was there; so were signers Richard Lee, who had offered the resolution that the Declaration be adopted; Samuel Chase, future Justice of the United States Supreme Court; and James Monroe, future President.

Three weeks later in the same room the Treaty of Paris was approved by Congress, thus officially ending the American Revolution. On that January 14, 1784, in the Old Senate Chamber, the United States became one of the family of nations. And here, on September 14, 1786, the Annapolis Convention issued its call for the gathering which met in Philadelphia the following year to write the American Constitution.

Thus, it may rightly be said that this State House witnessed the final acts of the American Revolution as well as one of the major events leading to the formation of a sound government of the United States.

The State House is divided into two parts. The colonial or original building can be recognized by its beautiful architecture, using plaster walls and wooden columns, while the annex or new part uses matched marble walls and marble columns. A broad, black line in the floor separates the old from the new. Early in the twentieth century, the State House was redesigned in such a way as to preserve all of its original colonial features, while adding a $600,000 annex to the west. This annex contains the present meeting places of the Maryland Senate and House of Delegates.

The following features of historical interest are found in the State House: Old Senate Chamber, with the original Charles Willson Peale painting of Washington, Lafayette and Tench Tilghman at Yorktown; Edwin White's famous painting of Washington resigning his commission; the Flag Room with many historic banners, including one of the Revolutionary era; and many portraits of prominent Maryland figures, including the four Maryland signers of the Declaration of Independence.

Opposite: The distinguished State House of Maryland (circa 1772), where General Washington resigned as head of the Continental Army, is the oldest Capitol still fulfilling its original purpose.

MASSACHUSETTS

THE STATE HOUSE *Boston*

The choice of the site for the Massachusetts State House, at the summit of Boston's Beacon Hill, was made in 1795. The cornerstone was laid on the Fourth of July that year by Governor Samuel Adams, assisted by Paul Revere, Grand Master of the Grand Lodge of Masons. It was carried to the site by fifteen white horses, representing the number of States of the Union at that time.

Designed by the Boston architect, Charles Bulfinch, the Massachusetts State House was completed early in 1798. It replaced a smaller State House which had been, for more than sixty years before the American Revolution, the seat of Massachusetts' colonial government. The Old State House, topped by the British Lion and Unicorn, was built in 1713 at what is now Washington and State Streets. From its balcony was proclaimed the American Declaration of Independence. Within its walls the Constitutional Convention sat during the first three months of 1780, reviewing and revising John Adams' draft Constitution for the Commonwealth of Massachusetts. Said to be one of the oldest public buildings in America, it is now used as a historical museum.

Facing south, on a sunlit day the present State House is a colorful sight with the sun bringing out the warmth of the red brick walls, the gleam of the white pillars and trim, and the brilliant reflection of the gold-leaf dome.

The original building has a 172-foot front; the height, from base course to pinnacle, is 155 feet; and the foundation is about 106 feet above the waters of the bay. The dome is 53 feet in diameter and 35 feet high. The original cost of the building was approximately $134,000.

The dome, originally shingled and painted a lead color, was covered with copper by Paul Revere and Sons in 1802. In 1831, the roof was covered with new copper and painted grey. At a later date it was painted yellow and, since 1874, it has been covered with gold leaf. World War II brought a temporary transformation to battleship grey. The dome itself has been rebuilt twice, in 1859 and 1897, when an effort was made to reproduce the lines and proportions of the original.

Extensive improvements have been made since the original construction, including five additions. The first, in 1831, was expanded in 1853-1855 and replaced in 1889-1895. Wings of white Vermont marble and granite were added from 1914 to 1917 when the State House was painted white. Lastly, from 1958 to 1960, the underground Archives and Records Building was added in front of the west wing.

When the General Court (legislature) met in 1898, the Senate moved from its old chamber, now its reception room, to the former House Chamber in the Bulfinch building, and the House occupied new quarters in an addition designed by Charles E. Brigham. The House, however, refused to sit unless the "Sacred Cod" moved with it. The wooden replica of a codfish has since 1784 (and perhaps since 1742) always hung where the Speaker of the House can see it.

The interior of the building is most impressive. From the ten-columned Doric Hall, next to the entrance, the Senate staircase Hall leads to Memorial Hall—often called the Hall of Flags. Side stairs lead from the Senate Staircase Hall to the Senate Chamber on the east, and the Governor's office and the Council Chamber on the west. Beyond Memorial Hall, the House staircase branches to the House on the west, and on the east to the office of the Secretary of the Commonwealth. The building also includes the State Library.

At the summit of Beacon Hill in Boston stands the Massachusetts State House. Governor Samuel Adams, assisted by Paul Revere, laid the cornerstone of the building on the Fourth of July, 1795.

MICHIGAN
THE STATE CAPITOL *Lansing*

On a spacious landscaped site across from the Lansing City Hall stands Michigan's four-story Capitol, topped by a dome and spire rising sharply to 276 feet. Including its porticos and steps, the building measures 420 by 273 feet. Above a limestone foundation, its walls are faced with white Ohio sandstone.

The design, in later classical Renaissance, was the work of Elijah E. Myers. An allegorical bas-relief, symbolic of Michigan's development, decorates the pediment high above the east entrance.

On either side of the Rotunda, a grand staircase rises from the ground floor to the fourth. Balconies look down upon the Rotunda's display of battle flags and its floor of glass blocks set in iron. At the base of the dome are murals of Michigan Science, Astronomy, Justice, Industry, Navigation, Education, Art and Agriculture.

The ground floor and first floor house various historical exhibits, including facsimiles of the four State Constitutions. The House and Senate Chambers and the executive offices are on the second floor, the judicial chambers and the House and Senate galleries on the third.

The Capitol's granite cornerstone was laid on October 2, 1873, and the building was dedicated in January 1879. It cost $1,510,130.

Two previous State Capitols were destroyed by fire, but after they had completed their governmental function. The Capitol in Detroit from 1828 to 1848, later the city's first high school and public library, burned in 1893. The first Lansing Capitol, a frame building, was replaced by a brick structure in 1853 and was demolished by flames in 1884.

Lansing became the capital of Michigan in 1848, succeeding Detroit eleven years after the State was admitted to the Union. Detroit had been the seat of government during Territorial times. The 1835 Constitution called for selection of a permanent State capital by 1847. After weeks of debate, the Legislature chose Lansing as the most accessible site, even though there were few roads and no railroads to the town. Its industry consisted of one sawmill. There was dense forest and a single log house.

Both the city and the government have since grown greatly. A Capitol Development Program calls for construction of a new Capitol west of the present structure, as well as several other buildings nearby to house much of the executive and judicial branches of the government.

The stately white granite Capitol of Michigan
is situated on a spacious landscaped site in Lansing.
The four-story building follows the classical Renaissance style.

MINNESOTA
THE STATE CAPITOL St. Paul

The Minnesota Capitol in St. Paul, sitting atop a hill, can be seen for many miles in most directions and it is well worth viewing. One of its many outstanding features is its huge dome, said to be the world's largest unsupported marble dome. The remainder of the building is of Georgia marble, except for the foundation and steps of native grey granite.

The structure was designed by the renowned architect Cass Gilbert, who received the contract as a result of a design he submitted in competition sponsored by a legislative commission. Gilbert later designed the Capitols of Arkansas and West Virginia.

This is the third Capitol in St. Paul. The first was built in 1854. Prior to that year, the Minnesota Territorial Legislature had met in the Central House in St. Paul. The 1854 Capitol was destroyed by fire in 1881, and another building was completed in 1882 on the same site. In only eleven years it had become inadequate to house the State government, and it was then that the Legislature appointed a commission to find a site and to erect a new building.

The Capitol Commission of 1893 employed Edmund M. Wheelwright of Boston to select from the designs submitted by the architects, and it was he who chose the Cass Gilbert plan. Gilbert supervised construction and all details, including decoration and furnishings.

The Legislature appropriated $4.5 million for the land and building, and ground was broken on May 6, 1896. The cornerstone was laid on July 27, 1898, by Alexander Ramsey, the first Governor of the Minnesota Territory.

On the first floor are State administrative offices and the Governor's reception room, with gold-leaf ceiling, marble fireplace and several paintings of scenes from Minnesota's history.

The Capitol's "grand floor" is the second. Here are located the Senate and House, the Supreme Court and several legislative committee rooms and offices. Four paintings by John LaFarge appear in the Supreme Court Chamber. The adjacent Justices' Consultation Room is a scaled-down copy of the room in Independence Hall in which the Declaration of Independence was signed. The Senate Chamber features historical and allegorical murals as well as figures of Freedom, Courage, Justice and Equality. In the north, or House wing, ceiling decorations commemorate the explorers LaSalle, Hennepin, Perrot and Duluth.

The Capitol's third floor contains the House and Senate galleries, additional committee rooms, and the main part of the State Library. Other offices are on the ground floor.

The building measures 434 by 229 feet. It is 223 feet to the top of the large marble dome, which is 89 feet in diameter and topped by a columned lantern with a gold ball.

The virtues of Wisdom, Courage, Bounty, Truth, Integrity and Prudence are represented by six statues above the main entrance. These are the work of Daniel

Chester French, who collaborated with Edward C. Potter on the gilded quadriga, "The Progress of the State," which stands at the base of the dome. The figure of Prosperity rides the chariot, while two young women guide the horses. The sculpture is of copper-clad sheet metal over steel framing, overlaid with gold leaf.

Inside, limestone from Minnesota quarries was used for the walls and ceiling; the main staircases are marble. A large, eight-pointed glass star, set in the first floor at the center of the Rotunda, symbolizes the North Star State. Along the walls of the second floor balcony are statues of Civil War heroes from the State.

A gilded quadriga representing Minnesota's progress since statehood stands at the base of the magnificent unsupported marble dome, said to be the world's largest.

MISSISSIPPI

THE STATE CAPITOL *Jackson*

Mississippi actually has two State Capitol buildings in Jackson—the Old Capitol, built in 1839, which is now a historical museum, and the present Capitol, which was built in 1903 and has since served as the seat of government.

Toward the end of the nineteenth century, the Old Capitol was found to be inadequate to house all of the departments of the State government. Construction of the present building began in 1900 and was completed in 1903 at a cost of $1,093,641, which was financed without the necessity for a bond issue or extra tax levy. It was designed by architect Theodore C. Link of St. Louis, assisted by his son, Karl E. Link.

When the new Renaissance-style Capitol was completed, the Old Capitol was vacated and for a number of years was allowed to deteriorate. By 1916, however, the need for additional office space had grown to such an extent that the Old Capitol was renovated and used to house a number of departments of government until the Woolfolk State Office Building was completed in 1949. In 1959-1961 the Old Capitol was restored.

The present Capitol, which underwent extensive repairs in 1916 and again in 1934-35, is an impressive structure, standing with formal dignity on a commanding terrace in the center of downtown Jackson. Its architectural style is classical Renaissance, and its design is similar to that of the National Capitol.

The symmetrical, four-story building, constructed of Bedford limestone with a base of Georgia granite, is 402 feet long from east to west, 225 feet wide through the center pavilion. A high central dome and lantern which rises 180 feet above the entrance is topped by a copper eagle covered with genuine gold leaf. It stands eight feet high and has a wingspread of fifteen feet.

The interior features blue Vermont marble on a base of black Belgian; the main Rotunda is of Italian marble with trimmings of jet black marble from New York and friezes and columns of scagliola. Elsewhere in the building, other varieties of marble are used.

Only four kinds of wood are used in the building— maple, oak, walnut and mahogany. The two legislative halls, finished with marble and scagliola, have rich, domed ceilings of oxidized copper, stucco and colorful stained glass.

All three branches of the State government are housed in the Capitol, with the Governor's office located on the third floor midway between the two legislative halls. The Capitol also includes a Hall of Governors.

Mississippi has had two other sites of government as a member of the Federal Union. A small brick church in Washington, Mississippi, the Capitol when the State was admitted in 1817, served until Jackson became the capital city in 1822. A two-story brick structure served in Jackson until the "Old Capitol" was built in 1839. During the Civil War, the State government met in Columbus and Macon.

The classical Renaissance-style Capitol of Mississippi, built in 1903, is capped by an eight-foot copper eagle which is overlaid with gold leaf and has a wingspread of fifteen feet.

MISSOURI

THE STATE CAPITOL *Jefferson City*

Missouri's white stone Capitol in Jefferson City is a relatively new building, completed in 1918. Limestone bluffs and the Missouri River form part of its impressive three-acre setting.

The magnificent white stone Missouri State Capitol in Jefferson City covers three acres atop the limestone bluffs on the south bank of the Missouri River and overlooks a wide expanse of Cole and Callaway Counties.

Occupied on October 5, 1918, after more than four years under construction, it cost $4,215,000, including furnishings and site. The Capitol is five stories high, 437 feet long and 200 feet in the wings. The height is 238 feet to the top of the dome and 88 feet to the roof of the wings. It accommodates both branches of the Missouri Legislature, the offices of the elective State officials, and many boards and commissions.

The grand stairway, thirty feet across, is said to be the widest in the world. The front doors are of bronze, each thirteen by eighteen feet—largest cast since the Roman era. Considered especially outstanding are the legislative assembly rooms, the historic and resources museums, the legislative library, the Governor's reception room and the House and Senate lounges.

Colossal reclining bronze figures by Robert I. Aitken on either side of the steps leading to the south entrance symbolize Missouri's great rivers, the Missouri and the Mississippi, while atop the dome is a bronze figure of Ceres, the goddess of agriculture, by Sherry Fry.

On either hand at the top of the grand stairway leading from the principal entrance to the third floor are statues by James Earle Fraser of the explorers Meriwether Lewis and William Clark, whose expedition up the Missouri River played a prominent part in Missouri's early history.

Throughout the building are murals and decorative paintings telling the legend and history of Missouri, including the much-discussed murals on the walls of the House lounge by Thomas Hart Benton, Missouri artist and grandnephew of the distinguished Missouri statesman of the same name.

Jefferson City was established as the capital by the Missouri Legislature at the end of 1821, a few months after statehood was approved. That year the State government moved from St. Louis to St. Charles, which served as the capital until the first Capitol in Jefferson City was completed in 1827. This was destroyed by fire in 1837, and the Cole County Courthouse was then used until 1840 when another Capitol was completed on the present site. This Capitol, remodeled and expanded in 1888, burned in 1911. Other buildings were used until the present Capitol was completed.

MONTANA
THE STATE CAPITOL *Helena*

On a gentle slope, surrounded by ten acres of spacious lawns, native trees, and other State buildings, Montana's Capitol faces out over the beautiful Prickly Pear Valley. A mile west of the Capitol lies Last Chance Gulch, now the City of Helena's main street, where gold was discovered in 1864.

Native Columbus limestone was used in construction of the main section of the neoclassical Capitol, which was completed in 1902. The two large wings, faced with native granite, were finished in 1912, making the present structure 425 feet long and an average of 100 feet in width. The cost of construction was $1,650,000.

A statue representing liberty stands atop the Capitol's central copper dome, 165 feet from ground level. Visitors entering the Capitol see the bronze equestrian statue of General Thomas Francis Meagher, fiery Irish patriot and Civil War soldier, who was an acting Montana Territorial Governor in 1866. The Capitol's interior, done in French Renaissance style, features flaring staircases, wide corridors and large rooms, as well as many murals and statues.

On the main floor are the executive offices. Most impressive is the spacious Governor's reception room in the east wing, decorated in tan, ivory and brown, with marble fireplace mantels at both ends, silver chandeliers, paneled walls and eight massive columns of English oak. In the entrance room to the executive suite is the painting, "Scouting for Custer," by E. S. Paxson.

Tennessee marble and tones of deep green, brown and gold decorate the corridors extending east and west from the main-floor Rotunda. The dome rises to a height of one hundred feet over the Rotunda floor and is enhanced by stained glass windows and oil paintings. Embedded in the terrazzo floor of the Rotunda is the Great Seal of Montana, containing a central representation of a plow and a miner's pick and shovel, and surrounded by mountain scenery and the great falls of the Missouri River. "Driving of the Golden Spike," a mural depicting the coming of the railroads to Montana in the 1880's, appears above the grand staircase, which is of white marble with bronze decorations.

In the west wing of the third floor are the House of Representatives and Senate Chambers and their committee rooms and offices. The east wing houses the Supreme Court, State Law Library, and offices of the Justices of the Supreme Court.

Constituting the largest room in the Capitol, the rectangular House of Representatives Chamber also is the home of the largest and most valuable painting owned by the State of Montana: Charles M. Russell's historical depiction of Lewis and Clark meeting the Indians at Ross' Hole, September 5, 1805. Valued by critics at $250,000, the painting measures twenty-five by twelve feet and is in place directly over the Speaker's desk. Montanans generally consider the painting as priceless, because of the Statewide affinity with both the subject of the painting and their native-son artist.

Spacious lawns, neatly landscaped and bearing many varieties of trees native to the State of Montana, complement the spartan grandeur of the neoclassical Capitol at Helena, completed in 1902.

NEBRASKA
THE STATE CAPITOL Lincoln

The present Capitol, the fifth used by the Territory and the State, is known as "Tower on the Plains." A 1948 poll of five hundred of the Nation's best architects rated Nebraska's Capitol one of the five best buildings ever constructed in the United States.

The building, designed by Bertram Goodhue, drew upon elements of architectural styles of ancient Asia, Greece, Egypt, Spain and the American Southwest to produce a structure strikingly modern yet representative of the prairie and the people of the State.

Built of Indiana limestone, it is in the form of a cross in a square, with four interior courts. The base of the building, 437 feet square, is two stories high. From this base rises the tower, 400 feet high, crowned with Lee Lawrie's thirty-two-foot, eight-ton bronze figure of "The Sower."

The building, furnishings and landscaping cost over $10 million. The actual construction, begun in 1922, took ten years and was carried out under the direction of William Younkin. More than forty varieties of marble, granite, limestone and slate were used.

A particular attraction are the doors to the Senate and House Chambers. Plain on the inside but deeply carved on the outside, the "Indian" doors to the Senate represent the "Red Man's Tree of Life." Inlaid, tooled leather on the House doors depicts the "White Man's Tree of Life." They are boldly colored in the style of the prairie Indians.

When the Kansas-Nebraska Act of 1854 brought Territorial status to Nebraska, a dispute broke out between the North Platte and South Platte sections over the site of the permanent capital. Omaha was chosen by the acting Governor, but soon after statehood (March 1, 1867) the Legislature, with South Platte forces in the majority, voted to relocate the capital. The little village of Lancaster was chosen August 14, 1867, and renamed Lincoln.

The first Capitol built in Lincoln was used from 1869 to 1883. The present Capitol was built around the second, which was then torn down so that the tower section could be erected.

"Tower on the Plains" is the nickname of the striking skyscraper which serves as Nebraska's Capitol.

NEVADA

THE STATE CAPITOL BUILDING
Carson City

Carson City is the only capital city Nevada has known. From October 31, 1864, when President Lincoln proclaimed the new State, until 1870, the Legislature met in many places in the city. In January 1869, a bill to provide for the building of a State Capitol was introduced in the Nevada State Assembly. After a stormy passage through the Assembly, the "Capitol Bill" was passed by the Senate and, with a somewhat shaky hand, Governor Henry G. Blasdel signed it into law. The authorized construction was not to exceed $100,000 in cost. Subsequently, over an eighty-year period, the total cost amounted to $332,383.97.

The cornerstone of the Capitol was laid June 9, 1870. Construction moved rapidly, and within six months the Capitol building was ready for the fourth session of the Legislature.

Despite the speedy construction, Nevada had a handsome and imposing building—a two-story structure in the form of a Grecian cross featuring Corinthian, Ionic and Doric styles. The interior was both lavish and lasting. Windowpanes of twenty-six-ounce French Crystal, double-arched sashes, vaulted columns and chandeliers hanging from ornate, scrolled centerpieces were just some of the touches. Alaska marble was shipped to California in twenty-ton blocks where it was cut, polished and forwarded to Carson City to be inlaid into the wainscoting, arches and floors of the building.

Since those frontier days, the Statehouse has been expanded. The first addition came in 1905 when a State Library, octagonal in shape, was built as an annex to the east side. Currently housed in this section are the Division of Archives, part of the Legislative Council Bureau and legislative meeting rooms. The building was extended to the north and south in 1913, providing larger chambers for the State Assembly and the State Senate and additional office space for State agencies. The 1967 Legislature approved construction of a new Legislature Building to be situated immediately south of the Capitol.

The Nevada Capitol at Carson City is a handsome two-story structure with the basic form of a Greek cross.

NEW HAMPSHIRE
THE STATE HOUSE   *Concord*

New Hampshire's State House, built in 1819, is constructed of granite blocks hewn from 20,000-year-old boulders.

New Hampshire's classic State House in Concord is the oldest in the Nation with the Legislature still occupying its original chambers. (Massachusetts and Maryland have older Capitols still standing, but their legislative bodies have long since spread into quarters of more modern vintage.)

Built in 1819 by Stuart J. Park for approximately $82,000, using prison labor, it has twice been doubled in size at forty-five year intervals—in 1864 and 1909. The first remodeling and enlargement was completed in 1866 at a cost of $200,000; the second, including fireproofing, was a million-dollar project. On the eve of its sesquicentennial, the historic structure and its 2.6 acre site were given a $600,000 facelifting.

The Granite State's granite Capitol was originally a two-story parallelogram. It consisted of a center with a fifty-foot front and a depth of fifty-seven feet and two identical wings thirty-eight feet wide and forty-nine feet deep. It was surmounted by a silo-like dome upon which a hand-carved, seventy-eight-inch wooden "war" eagle was perched peering eastward toward possible European hostiles.

Time has engulfed the tiny wings, and the State House now has a handsome Doric-colonnaded frontage of 128 feet and a depth of 165 feet. It also boasts an enlarged dome and a "peace" eagle of metal composition, erected in 1955 when its predecessor's tail feathers had "molted" beyond further repair.

Granite for the original State House was hewn from giant boulders on nearby Rattlesnake Hill, said to have rolled into Concord twenty-thousand years earlier during a glacial period. Blocks for the two enlargements were blasted from the bowels of the same hill, said by geologists to be some twenty million years in age. A marked difference in texture is plainly visible to this day.

The State House Annex, completed in 1939, houses more than twenty State departments and is connected to the Capitol by an underground passage.

When the Senate Chamber was redone in 1942, a series of murals depicting New Hampshire's history were placed on the walls.

On the lawn around the State House are statues of famous sons of New Hampshire: Daniel Webster, renowned Senator and orator; General John Stark, Revolutionary War hero; John P. Hale, statesman during the Civil War; and Franklin Pierce, fourteenth President of the United States.

During the Revolutionary period and early statehood (New Hampshire became the ninth and deciding state to ratify the Constitution, at Concord on June 21, 1788), several towns served intermittently as the site of legislative sessions. Concord was first used in 1782 and has been the only capital since 1807.

NEW JERSEY

THE STATE CAPITOL *Trenton*

The New Jersey State Capitol, a massive structure erected in 1792 and added to at various times, is located in Trenton on West State Street, near Willow Street. The grounds now have a frontage of about 650 feet on State Street and extend south to the Delaware River. The present area of the State House grounds is about eight acres.

New Jersey's seat of government was first organized at Nassau Hall, Princeton, in August of 1776 and then alternated mainly between Burlington and Perth Amboy, as well as Trenton, until the Legislature fixed the capital at Trenton by an act approved November 25, 1790, almost three years after New Jersey ratified the Constitution. Commissioners were appointed to obtain land and to erect a suitable building. The old State House was a plain, bare-looking, rough-cast building, and was erected at a cost of less than four thousand pounds. Numerous alterations and additions were made later and new buildings were erected adjoining the main one. On March 21, 1885, the front portion was destroyed by fire, and the Legislature appropriated $275,000 for rebuilding it.

The new rectangular, Renaissance-style building was finished in 1889. It has a frontage of 160 feet on State Street and a depth of 67 feet. It is three and a half stories high, with a Rotunda 39 feet across, which connects the new section of the Capitol with the original part. The Rotunda is surmounted by a 145-foot dome.

The walls are constructed of solid, fireproof, brick masonry, faced with a light-colored stone from Indiana, known as Salem oolitic, with foundations and trimmings of New Jersey freestone from the Prallsville quarries in Hunterdon County. The portico, doorhead and trimmings about the door are of the same material. The portico, with balcony, is supported by massive pillars of polished granite and surmounted by the coat of arms of the State.

A new Assembly Chamber was constructed in 1891 and a new Senate Chamber in 1903. In 1907, an addition was built on to the Capitol. The west wing was extended in 1911 and the east wing was extended a year later. Many improvements were made in the Capitol between 1947 and 1962, including a new front entrance and main corridor. Both legislative chambers were enlarged in 1967 to accommodate the expanded 1968 Legislature.

A more attractive neoclassical State Capitol Annex was built in 1931. The four-story, H-shaped, limestone structure houses the courts and several departments and other offices.

The New Jersey State Capitol at Trenton rests on an eight-acre site. The original portion of the building was completed in 1792, and subsequent additions have added to the complexity of the massive structure.

New Mexico government is centered in a circular building adapting the Pueblo kiva design.

NEW MEXICO

THE STATE CAPITOL   *Santa Fe*

One of the nation's newest, the New Mexico State Capitol also has one of the most unusual styles. Its circular design is an adaptation of the Pueblo Indian kiva and incorporates the Zia Pueblo sun symbol, which also appears in the State Flag. The Capitol's facade is in the modified New Mexico Territorial style.

The four-story building, costing $4,676,860 exclusive of furniture and accessories, was designed by W. C. Kruger and Associates of Santa Fe. It was dedicated in 1966. The Capitol's total area is 236,206 square feet.

The main floor of the Capitol is given over to the legislative chambers, spaced as segments of a circle. The Rotunda rising from this floor is twenty-five feet in diameter and sixty feet high, faced with marble quarried on the Laguna Indian Reservation and highlighted by the State Seal cast in its terrazzo floor.

Stairways, two public elevators and two private elevators for legislators and executive officials give access to the first floor offices, and to the upper two floors which contain offices for legislators and their committees, several executive agencies, the Governor, the Lieutenant Governor and the Secretary of State.

Construction began in June 1964 on the series of ever-widening circular structural elements consisting of rings and columns. Details include inner surfaces of marble quarried within the State, and movable partitions for future space requirements. The State Library, built during the same time, not only complements the Capitol but forms with it the first phase of a comprehensive Capitol expansion program authorized in 1963.

Santa Fe also contains the adobe brick Palace of the Governors, dating from 1610. It is said to be the oldest public building in the continental United States still in use, now serving as a unit of the Museum of New Mexico. For nearly three hundred years it housed the northern frontier governments under Spain and Mexico; the Provisional government set up by the United States in 1846; and the Territorial government after 1850.

The first Territorial Capitol was completed in 1886, but burned six years later. A second building was finished in 1900 and became the State Capitol when New Mexico was admitted into the Union on January 6, 1912. This Capitol was remodeled several times and expanded in 1952. It is now to be used as a State office building. With the new Capitol, it will form part of a Capitol complex.

New Mexico's written history spans over four hundred years, and in its buildings the tri-cultural course of that history is reflected. The new Capitol, while blending themes of the past, provides adequate facilities for New Mexico's future.

NEW YORK

THE STATE CAPITOL *Albany*

Started shortly after the Civil War, New York's Capitol took thirty years to build and today still ranks as one of the Nation's most unusual public buildings. Five stories high atop Albany's Capitol Hill, it commands a sweeping view of downtown Albany and the beautiful Hudson River Valley. The three-and-a-half-acre site, with almost as much ground area as the National Capitol, is beautifully landscaped.

The cost of the Renaissance and Romanesque building was $25 million, a figure almost unbelievable in those days. Chief among its distinctive features are the superbly finished executive and legislative chambers, swirling staircases and elaborate, carved stonework recreating dramatic moments in the State's history.

The building itself is a massive rectangle extending 400 feet from east to west and 300 feet from north to south, with walls 108 feet high and a large central court. The base of the outer walls, sixteen feet four inches thick, is reminiscent of a medieval fortress. The visitor immediately notices one of the world's largest staircases—100 feet wide at the bottom, it extends 166 feet eastward from the main building and rises to the main entrance on the second floor. Another superb stairway, the "million dollar" staircase inside the west end, rises 119 feet from the first to the fourth floor and is believed to have been inspired by the grand stairway of the Paris Opera.

Busts of famous Americans are sculpted into the Corsehill freestone. This work alone took many years to complete. Curiously included are some unrecognized heads, believed to be friends and relatives of the sculptors. The Albany Capitol has been in continuous use except for a few days in March 1911, when a fire forced the Legislature to meet in City Hall. The Senate and Assembly Chambers were spared destruction, suffering mainly water damage. Within three weeks, the legislators reconvened in the permanent Capitol.

The present Capitol is the second erected since Albany became the State's official seat of government in 1797. A stone tablet marks the spot where the first Capitol stood.

Until the move to Albany, New York City had been the capital since the break with Great Britain. However, the war forced the government to move to Fishkill, where the Provincial Congress met in a church; to White Plains, where the Declaration of Independence was approved July 9, 1776; to Kingston, where the first State Legislature convened in 1777, and to Poughkeepsie, where the U.S. Constitution was ratified in 1788.

The State Capitol in New York City, the old City Hall, which was torn down in 1812, had also served as the seat of government of the Province from 1699 to 1763, except for a few sessions of the Legislature held in private homes at various other locations. The last session of the Second Continental Congress was held there in 1788, followed by the First Congress of the United States of America in 1789, making it the first Federal Capitol under the Constitution. President Washington was inaugurated on its balcony. It was both the State Capitol and the U.S. Capitol from January 1785 to June 1790. The site on Wall Street is now marked by a statue of George Washington.

Opposite: The New York State Capitol in Albany is one of the Nation's most interesting and opulent public buildings.

NORTH CAROLINA

THE STATE CAPITOL *Raleigh*

The dominant feature of the heart of Raleigh is the North Carolina Capitol which is centered in Union Square, a delightful park-like area of over six acres.

When Raleigh was planned as a city, this portion was set aside as the site of the State Capitol. The first such structure was finished in 1794 in Union Square and was destroyed by fire in 1831. Construction on the current building was started two years later and it was finished in 1840. The architects were Ithiel Town and Alexander Jackson Davis.

Greek Revival was set as the architectural style and granite from a State-owned quarry near Raleigh was the main material used in construction. It is a cruciform shape, measuring 160 feet from north to south and 140 feet from east to west. The building is three stories high, and the top of its dome is 97.5 feet above the base of the Rotunda. The dome itself is copper that has attained a rich green gloss through the years of weathering.

The east and west facades have deep porticos. The Doric columns, five feet in diameter, and entablature are copied from the Parthenon in Athens.

Around the Rotunda are various historical tablets and busts of famous native sons. The circular, stone second-floor balcony is cantilevered over the Rotunda's first floor by nine feet. Massive stone stairways with wrought-iron railings lead to the second floor from the vestibules.

In the Capitol which burned in 1831 was a heroic-sized marble statue of George Washington by the Italian sculptor Antonio Canova. The designers of the present Capitol intended that a copy of this statue be placed in the Rotunda. Financial problems and disagreements about the appropriateness of the style of Canova's statue prevented this, but in 1967 the General Assembly authorized a private subscription of funds to execute a new copy, from the artist's original scale model, to be placed in this location.

Originally, the building housed all functions of State government: the offices of the Governor and Council of State were on the first floor, the Senate and House Chambers on the second, and the Supreme Court and library on the third. A separate building was constructed for the court and library later, and the new State Legislative Building, for the General Assembly, was occupied in 1963.

At present, the offices of the Governor, Secretary of State, Treasurer, and portions of their staffs are in the Capitol. The Senate and House Chambers have been restored to their original form and are kept as historic shrines by the Department of Archives and History.

Among the statuary on the well-landscaped lawns is Charles Keck's grouping of the three North Carolina-born Presidents: James K. Polk, Andrew Jackson, and Andrew Johnson.

Before Raleigh was chosen in 1792 to be North

North Carolina's Capitol is an outstanding example of the Grecian-style building often used in public architecture.

Carolina's permanent capital, the Legislature had been on the move since it first met in 1665—especially during North Carolina's first and third half-centuries. From 1723 to 1761, however, it settled down, first in Edenton and, from 1745, in New Bern, with only two sessions elsewhere. Most of the next nine years were spent in Wilmington. New Bern was used frequently thereafter until 1794, but from 1776 the early State General Assembly gathered also in Halifax, Hillsboro, Smithfield, Wake Court House, Salem, Tarboro and Fayetteville. It was in this last town that the U.S. Constitution was ratified on November 21, 1789.

The functional Capitol building of North Dakota at Bismarck towers nineteen stories above the surrounding landscape. Granite and limestone faced, it is called "Skyscraper Capitol of the Plains."

NORTH DAKOTA
THE STATE CAPITOL *Bismarck*

The North Dakota State Capitol in Bismarck is a modern nineteen-story structure noted for its simplicity, practicability and usability. The towering administrative section is 241 feet, eight inches high and 95 feet square. The length of the entire building, east to west, is 389 feet, its width through the center line of the House and Senate 173 feet, eight inches.

The steel-framed "Skyscraper Capitol of the Plains" is faced with Wisconsin black granite base and white Indiana limestone. The main entrance doors are bronze. In the ground-floor lobby and the first-floor Memorial Hall, the walls are covered with Yellowstone travertine and the floor with Tennessee marble. The stairway leading to Memorial Hall has steps and risers of Tennessee marble and walls of Belgian black marble. Memorial Hall is forty feet high; its columns and large window frames are bronze.

In early Territorial days the Dakota capital was at Yanktown on the Nebraska border, but the Territorial Legislature of 1883 named a commission to relocate it. Citizens of Bismarck offered $100,000 in cash and 320 acres of land as an inducement.

Bismarck was selected due primarily to its location on the Missouri River, thus insuring an adequate water supply. Also the Northern Pacific Railroad was anxious to have the capital on its main line at Bismarck. The town's cash donation was used in 1883 to build the old Capitol's first section, which cost $97,600. After North Dakota was admitted to statehood, Bismarck was selected as the State Capitol. Jamestown also received serious consideration but lost out at the Constitutional Convention.

The old Capitol burned on December 28, 1930. For the 1931 session, the Legislature used the World War Memorial Building in Bismarck. The new Capitol was erected in 1933-1934 and occupied in 1935. W. F. Kurke and Joseph Bell DeRemer were the principal architects.

OHIO

THE STATE HOUSE *Columbus*

The Ohio State House is considered one of the country's outstanding examples of Greek Revival architecture. However, for several years it appeared not only that the building would remain unfinished, but that the capital would be moved to another city.

The cornerstone was laid on July 4, 1839, and work continued on the twelve-foot-thick foundations. However, that winter, the Legislature repealed the State House act and for six years all construction stopped while the Legislature debated moving the capital from Columbus. Ultimately, in 1846, construction began again and was further spurred by the burning, in 1852, of the old State House.

The building was completed in 1861, twenty-three years after work had started. Meanwhile, eleven Governors had served in office, the State had had two Constitutions, six Boards of Commissioners had supervised the construction and five separate architects had been in charge at various times. In addition, Thomas U. Walter, one of the designers of the National Capitol, and Richard Upjohn, designer of New York City's famous Trinity Church, served as consulting architects.

The finished building was well worth the battle to overcome the controversy which beset the project from the start and lasted nearly to the finish. Eight Doric columns, each thirty-six feet high and six feet thick, are located along the main east and west entrances, with four similar columns at each of the north and south entrances. The cupola, which has a shallow conical roof, is 158 feet above ground level.

Double sets of massive bronze doors open onto the four foyers which lead to the Rotunda floor. A brightly lighted canvas, bearing the Great Seal of Ohio, looks down from the 120-foot dome. Circling the Seal are the names and inaugural dates of the eight Ohioans who served as President of the United States. The floor of the Rotunda is inlaid marble.

Until the Legislature in 1812 accepted an offer of forest land on the "high bank east of the Scioto River" at what now is Columbus, Chillicothe had served as the capital except for two years when Zanesville held this honor. Ohio joined the Union in 1803, with the first legislative session being held in Chillicothe. Prior to statehood, when Ohio had been part of the Northwest Territory, Marietta, then Cincinnati, had been the Territorial capital.

Doric columns six feet thick and thirty-six feet high dominate the facade of Ohio's Greek Revival Capitol, completed in 1861.

OKLAHOMA
THE STATE CAPITOL *Oklahoma City*

As might be expected from the "Oil Capital of the World," the Oklahoma Statehouse is surrounded by oil derricks and oil has been produced for many years from pools beneath the Capitol grounds.

The design of the building is Gothic but many features of Greek and Roman architecture are also apparent. Standing guard atop the five-story structure are great statues of lions which seem to protect the building and the State itself. Unlike most Capitols, it has no dome, thus making the lions even more dominant. There are British features about the architecture, too, because one of the designers was S. Wemyss-Smith, a native of England. Working with him was American S. A. Layton.

They used many kinds of stone, primarily white Indiana limestone. The foundation is Oklahoma granite.

Construction of the building in the northeastern area of Oklahoma City was started July 20, 1914, and completed on June 30, 1917, at a total cost of $5 million. The cornerstone was laid November 16, 1915. A dome had been planned but the excessive cost of steel during World War I dictated a change in design.

The building faces south but has entrances on all four sides. Above the doors on the south entrance is a reproduction of the Great Seal of Oklahoma cast in bronze. This door opens to a grand staircase which leads to the fourth floor. The north and south facades have Corinthian porticos, and the east and west facades have Corinthian pilasters. In the center of the Rotunda ceiling is a colorful reproduction of the State Seal, surrounded by a sunburst of leaded glass artwork.

The five-story structure of 650 rooms houses the Governor's office, both Houses of the Legislature and numerous other offices of State government. The building has approximately eleven acres of floor space. Alabama marble was used for the floors, Vermont marble for the stairways.

The Governor's office is in the southeast wing of the second floor and adjoins the Blue Room, a reception room used by the Governor and other dignitaries for various business and social functions. This historical room has recently been renovated to reflect the original décor of the interior of the Capitol.

On the fourth floor are located the legislative halls. The Senate Chamber is on the east side and is sixty-two feet long and fifty-one feet, four inches wide. The House Chamber, on the west side, is slightly larger. The galleries on the fifth floor overlook the House and Senate Chambers and provide seating for the public.

On the second floor in the west wing is the Supreme Court, the highest court in Oklahoma hearing civil cases. In the north wing on the second floor is located the Court of Criminal Appeals, the highest court in Oklahoma exclusively for criminal cases.

Oklahoma City was chosen as the capital city by vote of the people in 1910, but it required a decision by the

Oklahoma's Capitol combines Gothic, Greek and Roman styles. Two lions, which seem to stand guard over the building, flank the central pediment of the handsome structure.

U.S. Supreme Court in 1911 to settle the question of legality of the move from Guthrie, which had been capital of the Territory since 1890 and of the State since its entry into the Union in 1907.

Before statehood, the eastern part of Oklahoma was known as the Indian Territory. The Indian nations had capitals in several places: the Creeks in Okmulgee, the Cherokees at Tahlequah, the Seminoles at Wewoka, the Choctaw in Tuskahoma, the Chickasaw at Tishomingo. The western "Panhandle" of the State was a portion of that area of the Republic of Texas which was ceded to the United States in 1850.

Atop the white Vermont marble Oregon Capitol is Ulric Ellerhusen's statue of the "Pioneer."

OREGON
THE STATE CAPITOL *Salem*

The mastery of Ulric Ellerhusen, one of the West's greatest sculptors, is apparent throughout the four-story Oregon State Capitol, but the beauty of the building, its setting and its mountain vista share honors with the works of this distinguished craftsman.

The building of white Vermont marble is simple in design. It looks northward, with other State buildings on each side, over a beautifully landscaped mall toward the Cascade Mountains. Included on the Capitol grounds is Willson Park.

Atop the tower of the Statehouse, 128 feet high, is Ellerhusen's gilded eight-and-one-half ton, 42-foot statue of the "Pioneer," which can be seen for miles. At night, bathed in floodlight, it is especially outstanding. Other Ellerhusen decorations over the various entrances depict figures symbolic of Oregon's economy and history—the great eagle, salmon, wheat, a ship, a locomotive, a stagecoach, pack animals and a cow, sheep, horse, deer and buffalo. Ellerhusen also created the bronze of the State Seal which is set in the center of the Rotunda floor.

Marble, featured on the exterior, is also used extensively in the interior; rose travertine from Montana on the walls, Vermont black along the base and ramps of the great stairway, Napoleon grey from Missouri on the stairs and the Rotunda floor.

Among the Rotunda decorations is a sunburst with stars overhead, representing Oregon and the other States at the time of Oregon's entry into the Union in 1859. Four murals on the Rotunda walls show scenes from Oregon's history. Another four, on its industry, flank the stairs to the Senate and House.

Each legislative chamber also has a mural behind the rostrum, while friezes bear the names of 157 men and women prominent in Oregon history. Above the steps to the Senate Chamber on the east is the Provisional Seal (1834-1848); facing this is the Territorial Seal (1848-1859), which is atop the stairs to the House of Representatives. The seals were painted by Barry Faulkner and Frank H. Schwarz.

Specially designed furnishings are in the legislative chambers, the Governor's office, and the early American-style Board of Control Room, which is paneled in knotty ponderosa pine. The House Chamber's walls are of golden oak, while its carpet depicts the Douglas fir.

The Capitol grounds contain several statues—two large groups by sculptor Leo Friedlander are at the Capitol's main entrance, one showing the Lewis and Clark party led by Sacajawea and the other, a pioneer family on the Oregon Trail.

The present Capitol was begun in 1936, the year after fire had destroyed the preceding structure, and was completed in 1938. The first specially built Capitol in Salem was erected in 1854 but was destroyed by fire a year later. The Legislature met in the Holman Building during the twenty-one years before its next Capitol was ready. That Statehouse was completed in 1876 and occupied until destroyed by fire on April 25, 1935.

PENNSYLVANIA
THE STATE CAPITOL *Harrisburg*

The William Penn family is so much a part of the history of Pennsylvania that it is not surprising that the female figure atop the dome of the State Capitol at Harrisburg is nicknamed "Miss Penn"—but it is not true, as sometimes claimed, that it was modeled after Penn's daughter, Letitia. The bronze statue representing the Commonwealth holds a mace, symbolic of statehood, and also raises a hand in benediction. The Capitol was designed in Italian Renaissance and the dome is reminiscent of St. Peter's in Rome.

The building was dedicated on October 4, 1906, by President Theodore Roosevelt, and is the second Statehouse in Harrisburg. The first, which was built in 1821, was destroyed by fire on February 2, 1897.

In 1902, Architect Joseph M. Houston of Philadelphia was commissioned to design the present structure, which is 520 feet long and 254 feet wide. The dome rises to 272 feet. The exterior is of Vermont granite. Flanking the main entrance are two statuary groups by Pennsylvania-born George Grey Barnard. One represents man's spiritual burden, while the other depicts humanity advancing through work and brotherhood. Sculptured on the huge bronze doors at that entrance are the heads of the men responsible for the building of the Capitol.

Around the immense Rotunda are Penn's words:

There may be room there for such a holy experiment. For the nations want a precedent. And my God will make it the seed of a nation. That an example may be set to the nations. That we may do the thing that is truly wise and just.

Paintings by the Pennsylvania artist Edwin Austin Abbey in the Rotunda's recessed arches and circular panels illustrate the spiritual, intellectual, and economic advances of the Commonwealth. They are entitled "The Spirit of Religious Liberty," "The Spirit of Light," "Science Revealing the Treasures of the Earth" and "The Spirit of Vulcan."

Other paintings in the wide south corridor represent the religious influences upon Pennsylvania's history. These are by W. B. Van Ingen, another noted artist of the State. Carvings on the gilded capitals along the corridors represent some of the State's most outstanding persons of different national origins.

Tile mosaics by Henry C. Mercer are interspersed along the richly colored floor of the Rotunda and corridors. A grand staircase leads to the legislative chambers, off the second floor balcony. In the Senate Chamber are several historical paintings by another native artist, Violet Oakley, while those in the House of Representatives are by Abbey. Both areas have stained glass windows by Van Ingen. Also on the second floor are the richly furnished Governor's Suite, with more Oakley paintings, and the rooms used by the Lieutenant Governor.

The Appellate Courtroom on the fourth floor is used by both the Supreme Court and the Superior Court. Sixteen panels by Oakley portray the evolution of law.

From 1683, the year after William Penn organized the colony's first Assembly in Upland (now Chester), until 1799, Philadelphia was Pennsylvania's capital. There, Independence Hall, then known as the State House, was used from 1736 by the Assembly. It was also the first National Capitol from May 10, 1775, to December 12, 1776, from March 4 to September 18, 1777, and from July 2, 1778, to June 21, 1783. Here were signed the Declaration of Independence and the Constitution of the United States.

The seat of government was moved to Lancaster in 1799, and, in 1812, Harrisburg became Pennsylvania's capital city. The General Assembly met at the Dauphin County Court House until the first Capitol there was authorized in 1816 and occupied in 1822.

The dome of Pennsylvania's Capitol is reminiscent of St. Peter's in Rome. The bronze statue at its peak represents the Commonwealth, but is nicknamed "Miss Penn" after William Penn's famous family.

RHODE ISLAND

THE STATE HOUSE *Providence*

Although Rhode Island was the first Colony to declare its independence from Great Britain, it was the last to decide on a single city to serve as the State capital. It was not until 1900 that the seat of government was permanently fixed at the present capital, Providence.

Legislative history goes back to May 19, 1647, when the first elected Legislature met at Portsmouth. Many cities served as the meeting site until about 1740. After that, most meetings of the Legislature alternated between the Old Colony House at Newport and the old Capitol at Providence until 1900.

The cornerstone for the present imposing Capitol was laid on October 15, 1896. The building was not officially delivered to the State until 1904 but the Secretary of State took occupancy in 1900. Other State officials and the General Assembly moved in the following year.

The architects were McKim, Mead & White of New York, and the builders were Norcross Brothers of Worcester, Massachusetts. The grounds, buildings, furnishings and decorations cost $3,018,416.33. The City of Providence donated to the State 454,838 square feet of land adjacent to the land purchased by the State.

The length of the building is 333 feet and the depth of the wings is 133 feet. The diameter of the dome below the top of the gallery is 70 feet; the diameter of the dome proper is 50 feet. The height of the building to the top of the square base of the dome is 94 feet. The marble dome was the first in the United States and one of four in the world (Minnesota's Capitol in St. Paul, the Taj Mahal at Agra, India, and St. Peter's in Rome, the only one larger than this). At night, this dome is illuminated by a battery of floodlights.

Watching over the State from atop the dome at a height of 235 feet is a symbolic bronze statue of the "Independent Man." At the entrance are bronze statues of two great Rhode Island military leaders, General Nathanael Greene, of Revolutionary fame, and Commodore Oliver Hazard Perry, hero of the War of 1812.

A quotation from the Royal Charter of 1663 is carved in marble above the portico. Inscribed on the building's north side are the milestones of Rhode Island history: founding, incorporation, chartering, independence.

Around the inside of the dome is carved in Latin a quotation from Tacitus, which translated reads: "Rare felicity of the times when it is permitted to think as you like and to say what you think."

In the State Reception Room are four famous paintings. One is of General George Washington by Gilbert Stuart; the other paintings are of General Greene and Commodore Perry, both by Gari Melchers, and of Commodore John Barry by Wilfred I. Duphiney.

The State Library contains an excellent collection of books on Rhode Island, documents of the United States and the several States and books and pamphlets relating to history, political science and social science.

In the Governor's office and along the corridors are portraits of almost every Rhode Island Governor from colonial days to the present, while about the entrances are displayed battle flags and other relics and memorials.

Another historical relic in the State House is the original parchment charter granted by King Charles II, July 8, 1663, which continued in force (except for 1686-1689) until the present Constitution of the State became operative on May 2, 1843.

Opposite: Overlooking Rhode Island's capital city from a height of 235 feet is the bronze "Independent Man" on the dome of the State House.

SOUTH CAROLINA
THE STATE HOUSE *Columbia*

Just as Washington, D.C., was planned and built to serve as the Nation's capital, Columbia was established specifically to function as the capital of South Carolina, and the Carolina city even has claim to primacy because it was founded well ahead of the District of Columbia. In 1786, two years before the U.S. Constitution was ratified, the General Assembly chose a site "near Friday's Ferry on the Congaree River" to be the capital city. Later, the name Columbia was selected for the town and, in 1790, it became the seat of government, replacing Charleston, where an earlier State House had been in use since 1756.

Work on the present handsome Roman-Corinthian-style State House in Columbia got underway in 1855. The architect was Major John R. Niernsee. Five years later he reported that the project was nearing completion and would be ready within a year. Little did he realize that it would be nearly a half century before the building would be finished.

With the start of the Civil War, work came to a virtual standstill. However, to keep the quarry machinery and shortline railroad from deteriorating, the quarrying and transporting of the huge blocks of native granite continued and preparation of marble for the interior also proceeded.

When Union General William T. Sherman shelled Columbia on February 16, 1865, slight damage was done to the new State House. However, in the burning of the city the following day, the old State House, the existing seat of government, was demolished and much finished marble and granite at the site of the new edifice was ruined. So, too, were the architect's library and his drawings and plans for the new building.

After the war, it was decided to complete the building, but the advent of the Reconstruction period caused further delay, and not until 1869 was the roof installed and the unfinished building occupied.

Little additional work was done for some twenty years. Architect Niernsee returned in 1885 to resume work on the State House but died before the year ended. Finally, by the end of the century, the north and south porticos, with immense monolithic granite columns, and the copper-covered dome, a substitute for the originally designed soaring tower, were erected. Still later the great flights of steps were built.

In recent years, the interior has been renovated. The main lobby, its lofty embossed ceiling going up into the dome, features a bronzed statue of John C. Calhoun and real South Carolina palmetto trees, taken from the coast and preserved.

Above the triple doors leading to the State Library is a handsome stained glass window with the State Seal. The Library, to the rear of the main level, is centered with a Venetian glass chandelier, originally lighted by gas. Matching wrought-iron spiral staircases lead to the balcony.

In the east wing is the Senate Chamber, with its massive old desk of Honduras mahogany. The Sword of State hangs on the front of the desk when the Senate is in session. This was a personal gift of Lord Halifax, presented in 1951 to replace the original sword, which was made by a Charles Town silversmith and was in use from the beginning of statehood in 1776 until it was stolen in 1941.

Opposite is the Hall of the House of Representatives, also with its great desk and graceful proportions. It is paneled with Vermont verde antique marble. A lighted case displays the solid silver mace and gold burnishings, made in London in 1756. It is said to be the only mace now in use in this country which antedates the Revolutionary War.

On the lower level, with its vaulted ceilings and strong columns, are two recently renovated suites of offices, one for the Governor and one for the Supreme Court.

Construction on the Palmetto State's Capitol was begun in 1855, but the Civil War and Reconstruction period which followed delayed its completion until the end of the nineteenth century.

South Dakota's Capitol is built of raindrop sandstone and Bedford limestone in a modified Ionic style.

SOUTH DAKOTA
THE STATE CAPITOL *Pierre*

It is most appropriate that the South Dakota State Capitol should stand proudly on a bluff overlooking the storied Missouri River, famed as the highway to the frontier, because the State itself has been so much a part of the history of the frontier. Pierre, the capital city, is located on the site of what had been the capital of the Arikaka Indian nation for four hundred years.

South Dakota gained statehood in 1889 and Pierre was selected as the temporary capital. Fifteen years later, after much debate and two challenges by other cities, Pierre was named the permanent capital.

The first Capitol was a plain wooden structure just to the west of where the present building stands. The grounds around this building were prairie land with a deep gulch, but the gulch was filled and now is the handsome ten-acre Capitol Lake, fed by two warm water artesian wells. Visitors delight in this year-around haven for migratory waterfowl.

The exterior of the present State Capitol, started in 1907 and finished in 1910, is Marquette raindrop sandstone and Indiana Bedford limestone. The surrounding prairie furnished the boulder granite from which the basement was made. The original portion of the building was 292 feet by 124 feet and it is 161 feet from the ground to the top of lantern on the copper-covered dome.

The modified Ionic-style architecture, reminiscent of the National Capitol, is the work of Bell and Detweiler of Minneapolis. Including the art and furnishings, the total cost was only $944,000. The $400,000 annex on the north of the building was provided by the Legislature in 1931.

A wide sweep of gleaming white marble steps leads from the Rotunda and nearby Executive Suite to the legislative wings of the Capitol. The staircase, flanked by huge columns of concrete and marble, becomes an auditorium at Christmas and on other special occasions when programs are held in the Rotunda. The most impressive view in the Capitol is the dome as seen from the Rotunda, with sunlight filtering through stained glass panels in the circular walls of the dome.

The west wing of the legislative floor houses the Senate Chamber, patterned after that of the United States Senate. The South Dakota House of Representatives is in the shape of a rectangle, also patterned after the House Chamber in Washington. Galleries on the fourth floor provide excellent vantage points to view the proceedings. Supreme Court Chambers are located in the east wing of the second floor.

South Dakota's major governmental activities center in the Executive Department on the south side of the west wing of the Capitol. Here are the Governor's offices and conference room. One of the significant pieces of art among the Capitol's many murals and paintings depicting early-day history is the canvas "Spirit of the People" on the west wall of the conference room. It tells the story of the advance westward by the white settler and his family into what was then Dakota Territory.

Four adjacent State office buildings today complete the Capitol complex.

TENNESSEE
THE STATE CAPITOL *Nashville*

The popular Doric, Ionic and Corinthian styles are masterfully blended in the Tennessee Capitol.

Tennessee's State Capitol, overlooking downtown Nashville's Memorial Square, is truly a Grecian edifice. It has a Doric base; four Ionic porticos, modeled after the Erectheum in Athens; and Corinthian pillars in the lantern of the tower which resemble the Choragic monument of Lysicrates, sometimes called the Lantern of Demosthenes. The design was by William Strickland of Philadelphia.

Despite the Grecian styling, the crystalline, fossilated limestone gives it a true Tennessee atmosphere, as this material was quarried near Nashville, then hewn into six- to ten-ton blocks for construction. Tennessee marble is also used extensively in the interior.

The structure's cornerstone was laid on July 4, 1845. It was first occupied in 1853 and completed in 1859 at a cost of approximately $1.5 million. Including the porticos, the building measures 270 by 140 feet. A terrace seventeen feet wide surrounds the Capitol. The height to the top of the rusticated-stone tower is 206 feet; the tower alone is 79 feet.

Extensive repairs on the exterior began in 1956. A new copper roof and new windows were installed, the terrace and steps were rebuilt, and columns, pediments, cornices and entablature were replaced. Some 90,000 cubic feet of Indiana limestone were used in this work.

Inside, a double flight of stairs leads to the House and Senate Chambers on the main floor. The Hall of Representatives, 100 by 70 feet, has a ceiling supported by sixteen fluted Ionic columns. In the smaller Senate Chamber, twelve Tennessee marble columns support a twelve-foot-wide gallery on three sides. The ceiling is formed in radiating panels of lacunaria.

The Capitol's interior also underwent a renovation in the late 1950's. Excavating and finishing the ground floor provided more office and committee space. Ceilings and floors were replaced. Other modifications included a tunnel and two elevators.

As North Carolina's "District of Washington," as the "State of Franklin" and as a Territory, Tennessee Legislatures met at Jonesboro, Greenville and Knoxville. Except for one day, Knoxville was the capital from 1796 to 1812, and the first State Legislature met there in a frame building after Tennessee was admitted to the Union on June 1, 1796. Nashville was Tennessee's capital from 1812 to 1815, Knoxville again from 1816 to 1819, Murfreesboro from 1819 through 1825, and Nashville again since 1826. The earlier Legislatures met in log cabins, frame homes, a school, the Presbyterian Church at Murfreesboro, and the Masonic Hall at Nashville before the Capitol in Nashville became the seat of government.

TEXAS
THE STATE CAPITOL *Austin*

The Texas Capitol, which stands in magnificent splendor in the center of the City of Austin, is a symbol of the history and heritage of the Lone Star State.

Among the largest of the State Capitols, it was patterned after the National Capitol by architect E. E. Myers of Detroit in 1881. It is 566 feet, six inches long, 288 feet, ten inches wide, and towers 311 feet from the grade line to the top of the star held aloft by the "Goddess of Liberty." It is constructed of pink Texas granite donated to the State by the owners of Granite Mountain in Burnet County. Over fifteen thousand carloads were transported on a specially constructed railroad for the seventy-five-mile distance to Austin.

Ground was broken for the new building on February 1, 1882. It was dedicated on May 18, 1888, with the acceptance speech being made by State Senator Temple Houston, son of General Sam Houston, who was Commander of the Texas forces at San Jacinto, twice President of the Republic of Texas, United States Senator and then Governor of the State.

The House and Senate Chambers are located on the second floor on the west and east sides, respectively. On the same floor and between the legislative halls, the Governor's office is located in the front (south) center section and the Legislative Reference Library occupies the rear (north) center section. Offices and spacious living quarters for the Speaker of the House and the Lieutenant Governor are located to the rear of the House and Senate Chambers.

Originally the structure had 392 rooms and 18 vaults on the three floors and housed all branches and departments of the State government. Since then, eight buildings have been added to the Capitol complex for the Supreme Court and executive departments. Much of the first and third floors of the Capitol building has been partitioned into office space for legislators.

The history of the State under the six flags of Spain, France, Mexico, the Republic of Texas, the United States and the Confederacy is depicted in beautiful bright-colored seals inlaid in the terrazzo on the first floor Rotunda. These are flanked on each side by large inlaid names of the battles which were fought to win and maintain Texas' independence from Mexico.

Construction cost of the Capitol was $3,744,630, not counting the donated granite and the time of convict labor furnished by the State. However, the State paid only a small portion of the cost in cash. The basic bids were taken not on the lowest cost in dollars but on the lowest number of acres of public lands for which the contractors would complete the structure. The Constitution of 1875 provided that "Three million acres of the Public Domain are hereby appropriated and set apart for the purpose of erecting a new State Capitol and other necessary public buildings at the seat of government..."

The availability of these lands, upon which the building of this Capitol depended, results from an important circumstance relating to the annexation of the Republic of Texas to the United States. During its ten years as an independent nation, Texans voted twice in favor of joining the Union, but both of these early proposals were rejected by the United States. In the second of these offers, a treaty was signed in 1844 by which Texas agreed to cede all of its millions of acres of public domain if the United States would assume its $10 million public debt. This treaty was rejected by the United States Senate, with a major opposition argument being that the Texas lands were "worthless."

Thereupon, the Congress of the United States made a counterproposal that Texas pay its own debts and keep its public lands. This was accepted by the Congress of Texas, and Texas became annexed to the Union on December 29, 1845. This bad guess by the United States Congress enabled the State not only to pay for its fine Capitol with public lands but also to endow its Public Free School Fund with the remainder of its multimillion-dollar acreage.

The low bid of three million acres was submitted by a syndicate of individuals which included United States Senator Charles B. Farwell and his brother, John B. Farwell, Amos C. Babcock, Colonel Abner Taylor and Amos Taylor, all of Chicago. Amos Taylor served as the chief contractor. This land became the famous XIT Ranch located in ten Texas Panhandle counties.

Texas had earlier Capitols located at Columbia, Houston, Washington-on-the-Brazos and Austin. All were wooden construction except the immediate predecessor to the present Capitol, which was constructed in 1856 and burned in 1881, while plans for the present structure were being considered for approval.

The Lone Star State has one of the nation's largest Capitols, a majestic pink granite structure which took six years to build.

The Utah State Capitol, situated on a natural terrace three hundred feet above the valley floor, provides an impressive view from every approach to Salt Lake City.

UTAH
THE STATE CAPITOL   *Salt Lake City*

On a "bench," or natural terrace, of the Wasatch foothills three hundred feet above the valley floor, the Utah State Capitol can be seen from almost every approach to Salt Lake City. Although the site was granted by the city to the Territorial government in 1888, actual building did not begin until several years after Utah finally won statehood in 1896.

A Capitol Commission was created in 1909, and its members were appointed two years later. Architect Richard K. A. Kletting designed a mainly Corinthian-style structure, 404 by 240 feet, of Utah granite. Utah copper covers the 285-foot dome atop the four-story building, completed in 1915 at a cost of $2,739,528.54.

The two hundred rooms of the Capitol include chambers of the Senate, House of Representatives and Supreme Court. The Senate is in the north center section, with the Court in the east wing and the House in the west. The Governor's reception room—the "Gold Room"—is one of the costliest and most beautiful in the West. Offices of the Governor, Secretary of State, Attorney General, Auditor, Treasurer and the Departments of Health and Welfare, Development Services and Natural Resources are on the second floor.

Suspended by a 95-foot chain from the center of the dome, 165 feet above the Rotunda floor, is a 3,200-pound brass chandelier. A skyscape with huge seagulls is painted on the dome ceiling. The gull is referred to as Utah's "sacred bird" because a large flight of them once devoured vast numbers of crickets which endangered the settlers' crops.

The second-floor Rotunda also features larger-than-life statues of mining engineer Daniel Cowan Jackling, sculptured by Dr. Avard Fairbanks, and of Brigadier General Thomas L. Kane, by Ortho R. Fairbanks. Paintings by Gilbert White and Girard Hale, showing Utah pioneer scenes, are at each end of the Rotunda.

On the attractively landscaped grounds in front of the Capitol is a statue of Massasoit, the famous Indian of Massachusetts history, a copy of Cyrus E. Dallin's bronze original at Plymouth Bay. The Utah-born sculptor gave his State the original plaster cast from which the Capitol's bronze was later cast. Also on the Capitol grounds is Gilbert Griswold's Mormon Battalion Monument, commemorating the band of troops which marched two thousand miles from Iowa to California in 1846 during the Mexican War.

During the long wait for its present Capitol, the Utah State Legislature met from 1896 to 1916 in the City-County Building of Salt Lake City.

Salt Lake City has been the principal capital since Utah became a Territory in 1850. Fillmore, chosen in 1851 to be the capital, was used only sparingly in the latter 1850's by the Legislature, which preferred the Great Salt Lake City, as it was then called.

VERMONT
THE STATE CAPITOL *Montpelier*

The present State Capitol, dedicated in 1859, is Vermont's third in Montpelier, which was chosen as the capital in 1805. This majestic structure includes a central building with a Doric Greek Revival portico plus two wings that form a Greek cross. Appropriately, the exterior material is Vermont granite. The apex of the Doric portico rises sixty feet, and behind it, a gold-leaf dome and cupola add another fifty-six feet, nine inches. Topping this is a statue of Ceres, the goddess of agriculture, modeled after the work of Vermonter Larkin G. Mead.

Entered from the portico, the first story presents a striking appearance, with a black and white tessellated marble floor, deep double-sunk ceiling panels, and ornamented iron stairs. The columns in the lobby are Ionic.

Mead's bust of Lincoln faces the main entrance; his marble statue of Ethan Allen stands in the portico. Portraits of famous sons of Vermont line the walls.

On the first floor are the Hall of Inscriptions, various offices and the Legislative Reference Service. The second floor front houses the Governor's Chambers. In his office is an oaken chair carved from the timbers of the famed frigate *Constitution*—"Old Ironsides"—presented to the State in 1858.

On the second floor of the east wing, the elliptical Senate Chamber carries forward the Greek temple effect, with its fluted Corinthian columns and handsome ornamented ceiling.

The larger Representative's Hall is semicircular in shape, with fluted pilasters, Corinthian capitals, enriched entablature and paneled cove. Over the Speaker's desk is the State coat of arms, carved in wood by John A. Ellis. A raised platform in the curved rear of the hall accommodates the Senate during joint sessions.

Connecting with the west wing of the Statehouse is a rough-granite annex, used mainly for legislative committees. It was built in 1886 and remodeled in 1918.

Vermont's early history was one of turbulence. Although active in the Revolution, Vermont was not one of the original thirteen States but maintained an independent government for fourteen years. After it disposed of adverse claims against its territory by New York, New Hampshire and Massachusetts, it entered the Union as the fourteenth State on March 4, 1791.

At least ten different towns served as "capitals" from 1775 until 1805 as the legislators traveled from city to city for meetings. When Montpelier was finally selected as the permanent capital the first Statehouse was a wooden structure. This was used until 1836, when it was replaced by a granite building, which was destroyed by fire in 1857. At first, the Legislature appropriated only money for "repairs and improvements." However, the Governor's Commission decided that the State needed a new and larger building and consequently the present building was constructed.

Vermont's Capitol, following a Grecian motif throughout, is in the form of a Greek cross with a Doric Greek Revival portico and a majestic statue of Ceres, goddess of agriculture, on the dome.

VIRGINIA

THE STATE CAPITOL   Richmond

Virginia has been the center of much of America's early history, and the State Capitol at Richmond has been the scene of many of these events.

The first representative assembly in the Western World convened at Jamestown on July 30, 1619. The elected Burgesses, the Council of State and Sir George Yeardley, the Governor, met in the simple frame church on Jamestown Island. This structure, about fifty feet by twenty feet, continued to be used for about twenty years for subsequent meetings of the General Assembly, a term still used for the Virginia Legislature. The National Park Service has established that four Statehouses were used until 1676. All were destroyed by fire, and in 1698 the General Assembly decided to remove the capital to Middle Plantation, which was renamed Williamsburg in honor of the reigning English King, William III.

During the construction of a new Capitol in Williamsburg, the legislators met in the Wren Building, the oldest academic building in English America. The foundations for the Capitol were laid in 1701, and the General Assembly first met in the new but unfinished building in 1704. This was gutted by a fire on January 30, 1747, and a second Capitol was completed on the same site in 1753. After the removal of the government to Richmond in 1780, the second building was destroyed by fire in 1832. Colonial Williamsburg, a nonprofit organization financed by Mr. John D. Rockefeller, reconstructed the first Capitol, and the building is one of the showpieces of the restoration of Williamsburg.

On May 15, 1776, the Virginia Convention meeting in the Williamsburg Capitol resolved that the Virginia delegates to the Continental Congress should have Congress "declare the United Colonies free and independent states," and that the Convention should "prepare a Declaration of Rights."

Under the Virginia Constitution of 1776, the House of Burgesses was renamed the House of Delegates, and at the meeting of the first General Assembly under the Constitution, Thomas Jefferson proposed that the seat of government be removed from Williamsburg. The bill failed of passage in this session but was revived in 1779 and Richmond City was designated as the new capital. The seat of government was moved the following year, the General Assembly occupying a temporary building until the necessary land could be acquired and plans prepared for a new Capitol.

In 1785, the Directors of the Public Buildings requested Thomas Jefferson, then Minister to France, for assistance in planning the Capitol, and he employed a French architect, Charles Clérisseau, to assist him. Plans were prepared based on the Maison Carrée, at Nimes, which Jefferson called "one of the most beautiful, if not the most beautiful and precious morsel of architecture left us by antiquity." In addition to plans for the new Capitol, Jefferson sent a plaster model of the Maison Carrée, still on exhibit in the Capitol.

The cornerstone for the structure was laid on August 18, 1785, and the General Assembly moved into the unfinished Capitol for the October 1788 session. The

The aristocratic Statehouse in Richmond, once the Capitol of the Confederacy, was designed by Thomas Jefferson with the aid of a French architect.

new building established the classic revival, and many plantation homes began to use the columned portico.

The old hall of the House of Delegates was the scene of many historic events. Here, in 1807, Chief Justice Marshall presided over the trial of Aaron Burr for treason. Various Constitutional Conventions were held here, and on April 23, 1861, in this historic chamber, Robert E. Lee was appointed commander of the armed forces of Virginia. Nine years later, on April 27, 1870, a spectacular disaster occurred when the floors of the Supreme Court of Appeals, located on the story above, collapsed. Hundreds of people had crowded into the courtroom to hear the arguments as to who was the rightful mayor of Richmond, and the weight of the spectators caused the tragedy which killed 62 persons and injured 251 others.

Between 1904 and 1906, two wings were added to the original building, and through the years various modern improvements have been made. The old chamber of the House of Delegates has been restored and contains numerous statues and busts, including those of Jefferson Davis and Alexander H. Stephens, which remind visitors that the Virginia Capitol was also once the Capitol of the Confederacy.

In the Rotunda is the famous statue by Houdon of George Washington, one of Virginia's most distinguished sons. In niches surrounding the Rotunda are busts of other Virginia-born Presidents as well as the Houdon bust of General Lafayette. Portraits and plaques of distinguished Virginians, including many former Governors, are hung in corridors and offices throughout the building. The Capitol is a monument to the strength and growth of representative government as nurtured in Virginia from 1619 to the present.

WASHINGTON

THE LEGISLATIVE BUILDING *Olympia*

Standing on a trim green knoll amid the Capitol group complex of State buildings, the imposing structure known as the Washington State Legislative Building looks out over the City of Olympia.

From the dome of the Legislative Building, Mt. Rainier, Mt. Baker, Mt. St. Helens and Mt. Adams can be seen on a clear day. The snow-capped Olympic Mountains are visible from the lower portico. Rising 287 feet from the base, the dome is encircled by Corinthian-capped columns more than 20 feet high and is topped by a lantern 31 feet in diameter and 47 feet high.

Modified Roman-Doric architecture and Wilkeson sandstone give strength and charm to the building. Outside decorations, such as the oxen skull and wreath frieze and the cornice fringings, are carved in sandstone. Simplified Doric columns enclose the building. The main entrance colonnade consists of eight Corinthian columns each more than thirty feet high.

On the large bronze doors at the main entrance are reproductions symbolic of the major industries of the State, along with a replica of the first Capitol and an early homestead cabin.

The Rotunda is located in the center of the building, covered with an inner dome rising 185 feet above the floor level. Suspended from this dome is a bronze chandelier weighing five tons. This chandelier, twenty-five feet in length, is beautifully carved between the open fretwork. It hangs fifty feet above the Rotunda floor directly over a bronze reproduction of the State Seal, which is embedded in the marble and encircled by a wreath of oak leaves and acorns. At the four corners of the marble-faced supporting columns of the Rotunda are tall bronze standards, elaborately carved and fluted, which are exact replicas of early Roman firepots. The top of each contains a powerful light for illuminating the Rotunda.

Around the four balconies running between the supporting columns of the Rotunda are ornamental bronze railings decorated on each side with three reproductions of the State Seal.

On the second floor are the House and Senate Chambers, the former in Formosa marble, the latter in Escaletto marble. The Governor's Executive Chamber is finished in mahogany, maroon drapes and red tapestry. The chambers of the President of the Senate and the Speaker of the House are finished in walnut.

The State Reception Room is considered one of the most beautiful in the Western Hemisphere, with Bresche Violette marble from Italy, tapestried Martha Washington chairs and Tiffany chandeliers of Czechoslovakian crystal. Carpet and furnishings are in green, gold and red.

Foundations for the present Legislative Building were laid in 1893, but it was not until thirty years later that portions of that foundation were incorporated in the new building, which was finally completed in 1928 at a cost of $7,385,768.

Today, it is immediately surrounded by the Governor's Mansion, the Temple of Justice, the State Library and the General Administration, Archives, Insurance, Institutions, Public Lands and Public Health buildings. Close by are new State office structures.

When Washington became a Territory on March 2, 1853, Olympia was named its capital, retaining this honor when statehood was conferred on November 11, 1889. Originally, the State was to be known as Columbia, but Congress changed the name in honor of the first President of the United States.

A frame building—the Gold Bar Restaurant—near Capitol Way and Second Avenue was the first meeting place of the Territorial Legislature on February 27, 1854. The Olympia Masonic Hall was "home" to the Legislatures in late 1854 and 1855. A frame structure was then built on the present Capitol site and served as the Capitol until 1902.

In 1901 Washington State purchased the old stone Thurston County Courthouse and added a wing to house the Legislature. This building (now called the Old Capitol Building) housed all State departments from 1905 to 1919. Several departments still use it.

Opposite: On a clear day, Washington's highest mountains are visible from the dome of the Legislative Building.

The West Virginia Capitol is located on a beautiful sixteen-acre esplanade facing the Kanawha River. The 333-room building is considered by many to be a prime example of fine Italian Renaissance architecture.

WEST VIRGINIA

THE STATE CAPITOL *Charleston*

Both the West Virginia State Capitol and its setting in Charleston are among the most attractive in the United States.

The main building and its two wings are on a sixteen-acre esplanade above the Kanawha River, with a fine view overlooking the river area. From Kanawha Boulevard below the Capitol, a majestic stone stairway leads down to the water.

Many architects have called the West Virginia Capitol one of the world's outstanding examples of Italian Renaissance architecture and one of the most beautiful of the State Capitols. More modestly, Cass Gilbert, its architect, described it as ". . . classic in style and what might correctly be termed as Renaissance; the architectural forms are Roman with the single exception of the Doric vestibule at the ground floor on the river side of the building."

One of the most recently built Capitols, it was completed in 1932 at a cost of nearly $10 million. With a total of 535,000 square feet of space, it has 333 rooms.

Its steel skeleton is covered by buff-colored Indiana limestone. Of its eighty-six columns, those on the main portico are Roman Corinthian, the others a modified Doric. The golden dome, three hundred feet high, is illuminated at night.

Bronze doors open onto marble-columned foyers. Marble is used extensively inside: Imperial Danby for the walls, Italian travertine and white Vermont for the floors. From a fifty-four-foot gold chain suspended from the center of the dome's ceiling, a two-ton chandelier, 180 feet above the floor, lights the Rotunda.

The House and Senate Chambers on the second floor of the main section also feature impressive chandeliers, using 10,000 separate pieces of rock crystal. In the Capitol's showpiece, the Governor's reception room, the standout attraction is the light turquoise rug, which measures twenty-seven by seventy-two feet, is two feet thick and weighs one ton. The State Museum is located beneath the Executive Suite.

Two previous Capitols in Charleston were destroyed by fire. One was in use from 1885, when Charleston became West Virginia's capital city the second time, until 1921, when it burned. A temporary wood and wallboard replacement was then erected in forty-two working days. When this "pasteboard capitol," as it was popularly known, burned in 1927, the Senate met in a church and the House used the Court House, the City Hall, and the YMCA building until the present Capitol was completed.

Charleston and Wheeling had alternated as capitals until 1885 when the Legislature finally settled on the former city. In 1861, a pro-Union State government representing Virginia in Congress was organized at Wheeling. The northwestern portion of Virginia was then separated and admitted to the Union on June 20, 1863, as the State of West Virginia. Wheeling remained the capital of this State until 1870, and Charleston until 1875. Wheeling again became the capital but, in 1885, Charleston was named the permanent capital city of West Virginia.

The cruciform-shaped Wisconsin Capitol rests in a landscaped garden park situated in the heart of Madison.

WISCONSIN
THE STATE CAPITOL   *Madison*

Wisconsin is renowned for her lakes and the scenic beauty of her vacation lands, and the State's Capitol exemplifies Wisconsin's tradition of beauty. Located in the heart of Madison on an isthmus between two lakes, the Capitol is set on a landscaped garden square known as Capitol Park. Streets radiate from the square to all parts of the city including the nearby tree-studded campus of the University of Wisconsin.

The building, constructed in a cruciform, covers nearly two and a half acres. Each of the four wings extends 157 feet from the center portion, for a total of 438 feet across the building either east to west or north to south. The architectural style is Roman Renaissance with Corinthian columns on each of the four porticos. The pediments over the porticos are covered with allegorical sculpture.

Atop the core is a great white dome, built of granite on a steel frame and floodlit at night. On it stands the figure of "Forward," symbol of the State's Motto, with the right arm outstretched and raised and the left hand holding a globe surmounted by an eagle. The work of the celebrated Daniel Chester French, the statue is done in bronze covered with gold leaf and measures fifteen feet, four inches in height. The distance of 285.9 feet from the esplanade to the top of the statue is, by design, a few inches shorter than that of the National Capitol.

The building, which was planned and designed by the New York architectural firm of George B. Post and Sons, cost $7.2 million with furnishings when completed in 1917, eleven years after construction began. Durable white Bethel Vermont granite was used on the exterior. A variety of marble from such faraway shores as France, Norway, Italy, Algeria, Greece and Germany was used inside. Granite in contrasting colors was used for the floors, panels and columns.

Two hundred feet above the large octagonal Rotunda, on the ceiling of the dome, is Edwin Howland Blashfield's painting, "Resources of Wisconsin," nearly thirty-four feet in diameter. In the artist's words, it "is a symbolization of Wisconsin enthroned upon clouds and wrapped in the folds of the American flag. She holds the escutcheon of the State with the coat of arms of Wisconsin upon it, and in her right hand a scepter of wheat."

Immense arches open from the Rotunda to the wings, each of which has a grand stairway.

The legislative chambers are on the second floor, with the Senate in the south wing and the Assembly in the west. Other principal areas are the reception room in the Executive Chambers, the Supreme Court Room and the Hearing Room. All five are decorated with large symbolic or historical murals. Offices of the Governor, Treasurer and Secretary of State are in the Capitol.

The first permanent Capitol in Madison was used from 1838 until 1857. When it was outgrown, it was replaced by another, built gradually between 1857 and 1869 and enlarged in 1883. This suffered heavy damage from fire in 1904, but was repaired and used until the present Capitol replaced it.

Madison has been the State's only capital city, although the Territorial Legislature first met in Belmont and in Burlington (now in Iowa) before settling on a permanent location in what was then wilderness.

Originally part of the Northwest Territory, Wisconsin became a separate Territory in 1836. Reduced to its present size a decade later, Wisconsin entered the Union on May 29, 1848.

Completed in 1890 and Corinthian in style, the Wyoming Capitol has as its main interior feature a Rotunda with cathedral glass windows which cast a mellow glow on the circular hall below.

WYOMING
THE CAPITOL BUILDING *Cheyenne*

The Corinthian-like architecture of the Wyoming Capitol in Cheyenne is reminiscent of the National Capitol. The building was completed in April 1890, about two months before Wyoming was granted statehood on July 10.

Unlike many States which have had several Capitols, Wyoming has had only the present structure, although early Legislative Assemblies met in various places in Cheyenne after the Territory was organized in 1869.

The building of the present structure was authorized in 1886 by the Ninth Territorial Legislative Assembly, which directed that it should be erected in Cheyenne at a cost not to exceed $150,000. Plans and specifications were drawn by David W. Gibbs & Co., architects, in 1886. The cornerstone was laid May 18, 1887. The Tenth Territorial Legislative Assembly convened in the building in 1888, shortly before the central portion was completed in March of that year. The first wings were finished in April 1890.

As the State grew, the building became overcrowded, and in 1915 the Legislature provided for new east and west wings, completed in 1917. Today, the Senate is housed in the west wing and the House in the east. Each of the chambers has four large murals, the work of Allen True, which depict industry, pioneer life, law and transportation. The ceiling in each chamber is of beautiful stained glass, with the Seal of the State of Wyoming in the center.

The entire building is 200 feet long by 120 feet wide, exclusive of approaches, and the tip of the dome is 146 feet above grade. The first two courses of the building (above the ground) are of stone from quarries at Ft. Collins, Colorado; the building proper is of sandstone from the quarries of Rawlins, Wyoming.

The Rotunda, which is the primary interior attraction, consists of a circular hall, thirty feet in diameter. The distance from the floor to the lantern above the Rotunda is fifty-four feet. Cathedral glass reflects a mellow light throughout the interior, which is richly ornamented with plaster and elaborately turned woodwork. Three wide halls lead off the Rotunda—one to the main entrance and the other two to the east and west wings. The hall floors are laid with alternate foot-square tiles of white and black marble.